Heart of Submission

DEVELOPING A DEEPER
RELATIONSHIP WITH GOD

Sylvester Bell, III

KP PUBLISHING COMPANY

Copyright 2022 by Sylvester Bell

Heart of Submission: Developing a Deeper Relationship with God

All rights reserved. In accordance with the U.S. Copyright Act of 1976, the scanning, uploading, and electronic sharing of any part of this book without the permission of the publisher is unlawful piracy and theft of the author's intellectual property. If you would like to use material from this book (other than for review purposes), prior written permission must be obtained by contacting the publisher at info@kp-pub.com.

Thank you for your support of the author's rights.

ISBN: 978-1-950936-67-0 (Paperback)   ISBN: 978-950936-68-7 (eBook)
Library of Congress Control Number: Pending

Editor: KP Publishing Services
Proofreader: Frank Williams
Cover Design: Angie Adayl
Interior Design: Jennifer Houle
Literary Director: Sandra Slayton James

Scripture taken from the New King James Version®. Copyright © 1982 by Thomas Nelson. Used by permission. All rights reserved.

Some content taken from New Living Translation. Copyright © (Copyright Year). Used by permission of Tyndale House Publishers. All rights reserved.

Scripture quotations are taken from the Holy Bible, New Living Translation, copyright 1996, 2004, 2007, 2015 by Tyndale House Foundation. Used by permission of Tyndale House Publishers, Inc., Carol Stream, Illinois 60188. All rights reserved.

"Scripture quotations are from the ESV® Bible (The Holy Bible, English Standard Version®), Copyright © 2001 by Crossway, a publishing ministry of Good News Publishers. Used by permission. All rights reserved."

Published by:

KP Publishing Company
Publisher of Fiction, Nonfiction & Children's Books
Valencia, CA 91355
www.kp-pub.com

Printed in the United States of America

Dedication

This book is dedicated to my Lord and Savior Jesus Christ! When it appeared that my life was lost and destined for demise, Jesus continued to watch over me and created a path back to purpose through submission. The Lord helped me to see the value of His love and wisdom above anyone and anything. Living life without submission to Christ is an exercise in futility.

Also, I am thankful to my spiritual father and mother, Apostle Fred L. Hodge, Jr. and Pastor Linda G. Hodge. They accepted me even though from the surface I looked like an unlikely candidate to be used for Kingdom purpose; they put me on the path of submission and restoration. I love you Pastors and I pledge my time, talent, and treasure to support you in ministry.

> Thank you Jesus for my life, health, and strength!
> I dedicate this book to your glory and honor!

Foreword

I want to recommend this writing to all believers as a reminder of our sacred position in the Body of Christ. Our submission to the Lordship of Jesus is critical for the accomplishment of our assignment in the earth and the rewards that come along with it, but it must be chosen, submission cannot be taken. Pastor Bell has captured a revelation that he has lived out and role modeled for many years here at Living Praise Christian Church. This book is not information that he studied but a revelation that he has lived. This is a must-read for every believer.

Yours truly,
Apostle Fred L. Hodge, Jr.

Introduction

Learning how to develop a heart of submission should be every believer's desire. Jesus submitted to the will of His Father by dying on the cross for our salvation. If Jesus walked in submission, so should we.

Jesus taught us to pray, *Thy Kingdom come. Thy will be done in earth, as it is in heaven.* (Matthew 6:10) It is the will of God that we operate in the earth with heaven's system of rulership.

The system of rulership is KINGDOM and SUBMISSION. Kingdom speaks to authority and submission speaks to compliance to authority. God is unwilling to bend His ordained system of rulership because the introduction of any other system would be confusion.

Many fail to experience the involvement of God's support in their endeavors because they are out of compliance with God's system of rulership. Satan found himself an outcast in heaven because he failed to submit to God's rulership. One of Satan's primary strategies is to influence believers to refuse to submit to God's system of rulership, so they can fail as he did.

The revelation of submission became clear to me under the teaching of Apostle Fred L. Hodge, Jr. In my early years with Living Praise Christian Church, Apostle Hodge invited me to meet with him to discuss my purpose in the Kingdom of God. It was apparent that God had called me to serve as a minister in the church, but because of my negative past, there was work that needed to be done to move me into a position of compliance to God's system of Kingdom and submission.

Apostle Hodge gave me valuable advice, which helped me to begin my journey of a life of purpose. He told me:

1. SUBMIT your life to God's will
2. OBEY those in leadership
3. LOVE people.

He said, "If you submit to God's will, He will anoint you. If you obey the leadership, they will appoint you. If you love people, they will receive you." As you can see, everything started with submission. By following this sound advice, I not only redeemed time lost to my past failures, but I also began experiencing success and achievement in every area of my life. The most important success I have realized is to know that God is pleased with me.

Submission demands that we come under Kingdom Leadership. It is graced with the responsibility and ability to guide and cover those given into their charge. All those involved must know their place and function accordingly.

Many misunderstand the value of submission. Submission is not intended to demote you, but it is designed to prepare you for eventual promotion. The Word of God brings revelation to this established principle, *Humble yourselves therefore under the mighty hand of God, that he may exalt you in due time.* (1Peter 5:6) According to scripture, we can have great expectations of promotion when we embrace the principle of submission.

The Word declares, *Many are called, but few are chosen.* (Matthew 22:14) The reason the called are chosen is because they said yes to the call by submission. When you say yes by your submission, it sends a message to heaven that you are Kingdom fit and ready for duty.

Satan vehemently attacked Jesus regarding worship (see Luke 4:8) because Satan understood that submission is an expression of worship. For us to properly worship, we must be submitted to God. This concept will be explored and explained throughout this book. It is my opinion, that you will be convinced that submission to God is a wise choice.

Introduction

It is time for God's people to come to a higher understanding of the things of God. The Word declares, *And ye shall know the truth, and the truth shall make you free.* (John 8:32) Knowing the heart and mind of God regarding our conduct will help us to become increasingly more productive spiritually and naturally. If you want to walk in purpose and achieve maximum potential with your life, become educated and choose to practice the Word of God by walking in submission. Good intention is the first step to achievement, but execution is what will please God and put you in line for a higher level of leadership.

By reading this book, you will be invited behind the veil of revelation regarding "The Heart of Submission." Get ready for an eye-opening experience that will not only intrigue and enlighten you but will also prepare you to be elevated to your Kingdom place of purpose and destiny

Content

Dedication   *v*
Foreword   *vii*
Introduction   *ix*

CHAPTER 1 • Called to Submission   1
CHAPTER 2 • What is Submission?   11
CHAPTER 3 • The Power of Submission   23
CHAPTER 4 • A Man After God's Own Heart   37
CHAPTER 5 • The Set Man   57
CHAPTER 6 • The Support Man   71
CHAPTER 7 • Walking in Submission   85

About the Author   *93*

CHAPTER ONE
Called to Submission

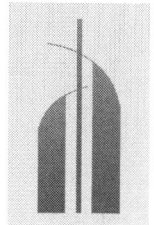

*"Submit yourselves therefore to god.
Resist the devil, and he will flee from you."*

—JAMES 4:7 KJV

SUBMISSION IS A GOD THING

The first thing we must establish as we prepare to develop a heart of submission is that God is the architect of the concept of submission. Submission is a principle that works in conjunction with God's system of unity and organization. Without unity and organization, the infrastructure for Kingdom viability would be in jeopardy.

Jesus taught the necessity of unity and submission to the Pharisees and others who were listening during a Kingdom moment of casting out demons (see Matthew 12:22-25). The Pharisees accused Jesus of using Satan's power to cast out demons, but Jesus declared that using evil power to combat evil power would be a function of disorder and ultimately cause the demise of an organizational structure.

Working in unity and having an organizational structure of leadership and submission is a priority for Kingdom success! God is very protective of His system of leadership and submission.

In heaven, Satan challenged God's system of leadership and submission. Because of his rebellious conduct, he was cast out of heaven and made an example for us to study (see Luke 10:18). I do not know about you, but I seek to learn from my mistakes and the mistakes of others. We must do things God's way!

God began the existence of mankind on the earth by creating Adam and Eve to become His subordinate rulers in the earth. The first communication recorded from God to Adam and Eve were instructions for Kingdom submission and leadership.

> *And God said, let us make man in our image, after our likeness: and let them have dominion over the fish of the sea, and over the fowl of the air, and over the cattle, and over all the earth, and over every creeping thing that creepeth upon the earth. So God created man in his own image, in the image of God created he him; male and female created he them, And God blessed them, and God said unto them, Be fruitful, and multiply, and replenish the earth, and subdue it: and have dominion over the fish of the sea, and over the fowl of the air, and over every living thing that moveth upon the earth.*
>
> Genesis 1:26-28 kjv

God understood that for mankind to have a life of success, He had to immediately establish an infrastructure of leadership and submission.

God started by giving Adam and Eve the authority to rule and have dominion in the garden. Jesus taught us to pray, *Thy kingdom come. Thy will be done in earth, as it is in heaven.* (Matthew 6:10) God is the creator of mankind, therefore He has the right to establish expectations for His creation. Besides all that, if God's system works in heaven, it can certainly work in the earth.

As a member of Living Praise Christian Church, I have observed the principle of leadership and submission at work in all areas of ministry. Our senior pastors, Apostle Fred Hodge, Jr. and Pastor Linda Hodge, have wholeheartedly submitted their personal lives and ministry to the lordship of Jesus Christ. They also expect those who serve under their leadership to have the same mentality regarding submission to God's system.

Each leader is required to undergo progressive leadership training and they are expected to lead and submit according to God's will. The general membership is also constantly given a healthy diet of leadership and submission training. Because of the culture of leadership and submission provided at the church, the ministry is progressive and adds value to the Kingdom of God.

Walking in God's system of leadership and submission has the power to re-direct your life from failure to success. There are many examples throughout the Bible of those who submitted their lives to God and experienced great success.

Moses submitted his life to God's authority and changed his destiny from being known as a murderer, to becoming one of the greatest prophets mentioned in the Bible. Esther submitted her life to God and changed her destiny from being known as a beauty queen, to becoming a deliverer for the Children of Israel. My life destiny was changed from being an absolute failure to becoming a man of God, a loving husband, and father, and successful according to God's standards. Change your life destiny by submitting yourself to God today!

WHO IS CALLED TO SUBMISSION?

The easy answer to our question, "Who is called to submission?" is everyone!

> *Submitting yourselves one to another in the fear of God.*
> EPHESIANS 5:21 KJV

The context of this passage of scripture speaks to relationships in marriage, but it can also be applied from person to person. Submission helps to eliminate disorganization and confusion.

In relationships, each person has a part to play to ensure that harmony and the overall purpose of the relationship are achieved. God requires His children to submit to Him so that He can help us experience a joyful and productive lifestyle. After we present ourselves to God for rulership, we then receive love, wisdom, and guidance for living with one another.

Leadership and submission shift based on responsibility (we will discuss this later in the book). This shifting mechanism helps us to assume our role in every relationship we encounter. Many times, when there is schism and/or division in relationships, it is because someone has violated the principle of submission. Leadership is great, but submission is also needed for the relationship to function properly.

We are called to submit to various forms of leadership.

> *Let every soul be subject unto the higher powers. For there is no power but of God: the powers that be are ordained of God. Whosoever, therefore, resisteth the power, resisteth the ordinance of God: and they that resist shall receive to themselves damnation.*
>
> ROMANS 13:1-2 KJV

The bedrock of spiritual and natural organization depends on us embracing the principle of submission. The angels practice submission when interacting with God and with one another.

In a beautiful story, Jacob was resting at a place called Bethel. He received a vision of angels using a stairway to ascend to heaven and to descend to the earth. The angels ascended to heaven to receive assignments from God, and then they descended to execute His will on the earth.

God requires those who are called by Him, to be ready to receive His instructions and perform His will quickly, without question. The angelic host understands this requirement; therefore, they provide a good example for us to follow.

Based on the scripture in Romans, God has instituted this same principle of submission in the secular dealings of mankind. We are called to submit to government leaders, city officials, and others who are called to lead on the earth. There is great responsibility given to those in leadership, and they have been given the grace necessary to function in their roles.

Good leaders are approved and rewarded by God. Bad leaders are disapproved and rebuked by God. It may appear that bad leaders get away with misconduct but be assured God holds them accountable for their actions. Those who abuse the power of leadership to oppress others will ultimately be subject to judgment. It is imperative that the church practice godly submission to leadership. Jesus is the Head of the Church, and He has appointed (and anointed) selected people to serve in church leadership.

> *For the husband is the head of the wife, even as Christ is the head of the church: and he is the saviour of the body.*
> EPHESIANS 5:23 KJV

There is peace and confidence in knowing that Jesus Christ oversees the church! Jesus brings with Him the necessary components for good leadership: love, power, and godly wisdom. Everything that Jesus does is based in godliness. Many are worried because of the state of the church, as seen through natural eyes. Be assured that God is in control and submission to the Leader of the church (Jesus Christ) is a wise choice. He has appointed and anointed selected people to assist Him with leading the church (apostles, prophets, evangelists, pastors, teachers, see Ephesians 4:11-13). These ministry gifts are subject to the leadership of Jesus Christ, and therefore are worthy of great respect.

Submission to Jesus and His leadership team will put you in position for godly provision, protection, and promotion.

A GOOD LEADER TO FOLLOW

The target for true submission is righteous leadership. One of the biggest problems that negatively affect submission is finding someone worthy of submission. Bad leadership is an obstacle to the heart of submission. It has been said, "Lead well and they will submit to you"

God has created in all of us an innate desire to find good leadership so that we can join ourselves to a cause. We were created to be community beings; therefore, it is imperative that we be connected to others who are progressive and good leaders.

The greatest leadership you will ever encounter is that which is displayed by the Godhead (the Father, the Son, and the Holy Spirit). The Kingdom of God is founded on great leadership. Each member of the Godhead functions on supernatural levels of leadership. There are several scriptures that provide proof-text regarding Godhead leadership:

> *Teach me to do thy will; for thou art my God:*
> *thy spirit is good; lead me into the land of uprightness.*
> PSALMS 143:10 KJV

> *Thus, saith the LORD, thy Redeemer, the Holy One of Israel;*
> *I am the LORD thy God which teacheth thee to profit,*
> *which leadeth thee by the way that thou shouldest go.*
> ISAIAH 48:17 KJV

> *Then answered Jesus and said unto them, Verily, verily, I say unto you,*
> *The Son can do nothing of himself, but what he seeth the Father do: for*
> *what things soever he doeth, these also doeth the Son likewise.*
> JOHN 5:19 KJV

Howbeit when he, the Spirit of truth, is come, he will guide you into all truth: for he shall not speak of himself; but whatsoever he shall hear, that shall he speak: and he will shew you things to come.

JOHN 16:13 KJV

Each one of these scriptures speaks to the nature and leadership functionality of the Godhead. We are blessed to have the opportunity to submit ourselves to God. God will not force you to submit your life to Him, but He will strongly encourage you to submit to Him. When dealing with the Children of Israel, God put before them a life-altering proposition,

I call heaven and earth to record this day against you, that I have set before you life and death, blessing and cursing: therefore choose life, that both thou and thy seed may live.

DEUTERONOMY 30:19 KJV

The Children of Israel were given the opportunity to choose to submit to God and live or refuse to submit to God and die. Why would they die if they did not submit their lives to God? Because a person not submitted to God is relegated to living by their own resources and power. God is omnipotent, which affords Him access to unlimited resources and power. Man without God, is impotent, which subjects him to limited resources and power. Ok, you tell me, which is the best choice?

Those who are in authority must practice good Kingdom leadership principles. How you treat God's people will affect your ability to experience the full "Blessing of Leadership" and motivate others to submit to you.

Moses had an anger problem which caused him to mistreat others. He killed a man and verbally insulted God's people. His actions kept him from experiencing the full "blessing of leadership." He was allowed to see the Promised Land but not allowed to enter it. *Also the LORD was angry with me for your sakes, saying, Thou also shalt not go in thither.* (Deuteronomy 1:37 KJV) Daniel, on the other hand, benefited greatly by practicing godly leadership principles.

> *It pleased Darius to set over the kingdom a hundred and twenty princes, which should be over the whole kingdom; And over these three presidents; of whom Daniel was first: that the princes might give accounts unto them, and the king should have no damage. Then this Daniel was preferred above the presidents and princes because an excellent spirit was in him, and the king thought to set him over the whole realm.*
> Daniel 6:1-3 KJV

Daniel demonstrated what was defined as an "excellent spirit." An excellent spirit demonstrates superior leadership skills, expressed wisdom, and manifested integrity. These characteristics work together to help make you an appealing leader worth following. Daniel obviously was connected to the heart of God, which helped him to express good leadership practices in his life and work.

The Bible declares that it is God who creates a leader, *It is God who judges: He brings one down, he exalts another.* (Psalms 75:7 KJV) The goodness of God is that when He calls you to a position, He will also supply you with the ability to perform the task.

What are some of the attributes needed to be a good leader?

The Love of God – Helps you maintain righteous motives and righteous interaction with others.

The Wisdom of God – Helps you make decisions based on truth.

The Help of God – Helps you overcome the challenges that disrupt, deceive, and ultimately disconnect you, and others submitted to you, from fulfilling God's will.

I have been a leader in my spiritual and secular life and learned through my experience that others willingly submit to my leadership when I practice good, godly leadership principles. One basic truth I have learned about leadership is that good leaders are first good followers.

TESTIFY

I was blessed by God to connect to great leaders (Apostle Fred L. Hodge, Jr. and Pastor Linda G. Hodge). I made the decision to submit to their leadership and join them in executing Kingdom vision at Living Praise Christian Church.

I have not only followed what they have taught me at (LPCC) regarding submission and leadership, but I also observed their lifestyle closely (some things are caught, not taught). I came to discover that they are not only great leaders but they are truly submitted to God and to their spiritual father in the faith. They taught me that no matter how high you rise; you must always maintain a secure foundation of submission to support your ascension

When others were chasing titles, fortune, and fame, they chased the heart of God through submission. The beautiful lesson I learned is that we must make it a priority to chase after the will of God for our lives.

Praise Break: Glory to God!

In summary, lead well and others will follow.

PRAYER

Father God, I hear the call to walk in accordance to Your will by submission. Please help me to submit to your will and your way by the Holy Spirit. I give You my heart, my soul, and my body. I love You and I look forward to a life of peace, joy, and happiness. Breathe in me Your purpose and Your will for Kingdom purpose. I submit my life to You and I ask for all these things in Jesus name. Amen!

CHAPTER TWO

What is Submission?

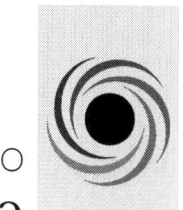

"Submit yourselves to every ordinance of man for the Lord's sake: whether it be to the king, as supreme; Or unto governors, as unto them that are sent by him for the punishment of evildoers, and for the praise of them that do well."

1 PETER 2:13-14 KJV

In Chapter One, we discussed good reasons for you to seek after "A Heart of Submission." The main point of the chapter provides facts and revelation that God requires that we submit ourselves to Him, and to those who are in authority. Hopefully, your interest is peaked to learn more about submission.

In Chapter Two, I want to provide you with a biblical definition and Kingdom revelation regarding the concept of submission. Many misunderstand the true meaning of submission. The natural concept of submission is good but limited. We must understand what God has established as Kingdom submission so that we will operate in line with His will. The Bible says that we must seek to get an understanding (see Proverbs 4:7) so we will have the knowledge necessary to help us make quality decisions.

First, let us look at natural submission.

WHAT IS NATURAL SUBMISSION?

The dictionary defines submission as the following:

4. An act or instance of submitting
5. The condition of having submitted
6. Submissive conduct or attitude

These are all great definitions that help us to operate in a governmental system for accomplishing purpose in the earth. The application of earthly submission speaks to the concept of leader and follower infrastructure. The corporate structure that is utilized in the earth, is a direct spin-off from what God established in heaven. What makes the concept of submission possible is the act of submitting.

The dictionary defines the word submit as the following:

1. To give over or yield to the power or authority of another.
2. To subject to some kind of treatment or influence.
3. To defer to another's judgment, opinion, decision.

The core of submitting has to do with you using your will, to defer to the will of another. To me this concept is asking you to make a valuable investment of your time, talent, and resources. For me to put myself in a position to submit to another, there are questions that must be answered:

a) Does the person or organization stand in opposition to God's will?
b) Is this an immoral person or organization?
c) Is it unsafe for me to place myself in submission to this person or organization?

These questions are subject to whether you have the power to choose or not in a particular situation. In some instances, you may not have a choice in the matter.

If the answer to these questions is "No," then the person or organization is a good candidate for my submission.

Secondly, let us look at Kingdom (or spiritual) submission.

WHAT IS KINGDOM SUBMISSION?

Kingdom submission, like natural submission, is based on submitting your life to the power or authority of another. But Kingdom submission introduces another dimension of the submission experience. For me to understand the difference between natural submission and Kingdom submission, I asked the Lord, "What is the difference between the two?" I love God because the Bible declares, *Delight thyself also in the LORD; and he shall give thee the desires of thine heart.* (Psalms 37:4) My desire to learn prompted the Lord to open a channel of revelation.

The Lord made it so plain to me regarding my question that I was motivated to a place of worship. The Lord revealed to me the following truth: Natural submission leads to COMPLIANCE, but Kingdom submission leads to CONNECTION.

Now, I understand the significance of why Jesus spent time to ask His disciples the question regarding His identity. Let us look into the story:

> *"When Jesus came into the coasts of Caesarea Philippi, he asked his disciples, saying, Whom do men say that I the Son of man am? And they said, Some say that thou art John the Baptist: some, Elias; and others, Jeremias, or one of the prophets. He saith unto them, But whom say ye that I am? And Simon Peter answered and said, Thou art the Christ, the Son of the living God. And Jesus answered and said unto him,*

HEART OF SUBMISSION

Blessed art thou, Simon Barjona: for flesh and blood hath not revealed it unto thee, but my Father which is in heaven. And I say also unto thee, that thou art Peter, and upon this rock I will build my church; and the gates of hell shall not prevail against it.
MATTHEW 16:13-18 KJV

This story begins with Jesus doing a knowledge identity check with His disciples. Jesus, understanding that He was close to the fulfillment of His time in the earth, wanted to make sure His disciples were prepared and equipped for their turn to carry the Baton of Purpose. For them to accomplish Kingdom purpose, they needed to be connected to Him by Kingdom submission.

Let us unpack the story . . .

Jesus asked the disciples, *"Whom do men say that I am?"* the answer returned that men see you as an evangelist, prophet, or spiritual leader. That is a good try, but it is limited to the experience of men who cannot see with spiritual eyes. This lets me know that men have the propensity to submit to leadership merely by having an earthly understanding. This is not good enough for Kingdom purpose!

You can be a good church member, but not be connected to the God of the church,

Oh my!

Jesus heard their answer, so He took the opportunity to prove a point. He differentiated between the knowledge of men who are not submitted to God with that of men who are submitted to God by asking the disciples,

"But, whom say ye that I am?"

Immediately, the supernatural revelation of God came upon Simon Peter and he said, *"Thou art the Christ, the Son of the living God."*

Jesus heard Simon Peter's answer, He became excited and declared, *"Blessed art thou, Simon Barjona!"*

Why is Simon Barjona blessed? Because he is a living example of Kingdom submission. Simon is blessed because He received revelation from God that is reserved for those who are CONNECTED to God by Kingdom submission.

Jesus is connected to the Father God; the disciples are connected to Jesus. The disciples are included in the Family of God. One of the benefits of being a family member in the Kingdom of God is that you are eligible to receive supernatural revelation. When you can properly SEE and PERCEIVE the identity of God and His leaders, it will become the catalyst for Kingdom submission.

Kingdom submission will help you withstand anything that the enemy or the pressures of life introduce. These pressures could potentially disconnect you from God or His leader. Stay connected!!!

Every believer should seek to walk in Kingdom submission to God and to those who have been given to them as Kingdom leaders (parents, pastors, righteous leaders, etc.) The Bible is filled with Kingdom relationships that demonstrate Kingdom submission at work.

The relationship between Moses and Joshua is a good example of Kingdom submission. Joshua submitted himself to Moses and received a supernatural grace transfer of provision, protection, and promotion. For instance, Moses was called by God to ascend Mt. Sinai and receive tablets of stone. God had forbidden any man or animal to approach the mountain or to touch it. The penalty was death.

> *And the LORD said unto Moses, Come up to me into the mount, and be there: and I will give thee tables of stone, and a law, and commandments*

which I have written; that thou mayest teach them. And Moses rose up, and his minister Joshua: and Moses went up into the mount of God. And he said unto the elders, Tarry ye here for us until we come again unto you: and, behold, Aaron and Hur are with you: if any man have any matters to do, let him come unto them.

Exodus 24:12-14 kjv

The reason Joshua was not killed was because of his connection through Kingdom submission to Moses. The power of Kingdom submission protected him. The grace on Moses' life covered the life of Joshua. God honors Kingdom submission so He has written a loophole in the spiritual realm that Kingdom submission allows privileges that are only experienced by the submitted.

Those who are connected are best protected!

Because of Kingdom submission, Joshua was not only allowed access to special places of privilege but he was also given the honor to become the next leader of Israel after Moses.

Another great example of Kingdom submission is the story of Naomi and Ruth. Naomi was Ruth's mother-in-law. Because of a traumatic situation, Naomi requested that Ruth returns to her people. But Ruth did not want to disconnect from Naomi, so Ruth activated the power of Kingdom submission through the power of choice.

And Naomi said, Turn again, my daughters: why will ye go with me? are there yet any more sons in my womb, that they may be your husbands? Turn again, my daughters, go your way; for I am too old to have an husband. If I should say, I have hope, if I should have an husband also tonight, and should also bear sons; Would ye tarry for them till they were

> *grown? would ye stay for them from having husbands? nay, my daughters; for it grieveth me much for your sakes that the hand of the LORD is gone out against me. And they lifted up their voice and wept again: and Orpah kissed her mother in law, but Ruth clave unto her. And she said, Behold, thy sister in law is gone back unto her people, and unto her gods: return thou after thy sister in law. And Ruth said, Intreat me not to leave thee, or to return from following after thee: for whither thou goest, I will go; and where thou lodgest, I will lodge: thy people shall be my people, and thy God my God: Where thou diest, will I die, and there will I be buried: the LORD do so to me, and more also if ought but death part thee and me.*
>
> RUTH 1:11-17 KJV

This story exemplifies natural submission and Kingdom submission. Ruth had the opportunity to separate from Naomi, due to the traumatic situation, but Ruth chose to secure her connection to Naomi with a heart of submission. Ruth makes a declaration to Naomi, "I will not disconnect from you, and to prove my submission to you, here are the following submission pledges:

- Where you go, I will go
- Where you live, I will live
- Your people, will be my people
- Your God, will be my God
- Where you are buried, I will be buried

Ruth was serious! Ruth submitted to Naomi naturally and spiritually. This level of submission will even supersede rejection from your leader. Naomi urged Ruth to go back to her people, but Ruth declined to disconnect. I surmise that Ruth received a revelation that Naomi was her

God-given leader. When you have an inward revelation of who your God-given leader is, you have the power to overcome the disconnecting factors that come to separate you from your leader. Stay connected!

As we can see, when you walk in Kingdom submission there are special privileges applied to your life. Also, Kingdom submission has the power to keep you connected to God and to your spiritual leader in difficult times. Kingdom submission requires a true commitment.

Commitment is like cement; both have the power to bind

Those who commit to staying connected by Kingdom submission will not be denied!

TESTIFY

I remember a time in my life that demonstrated the benefit of Kingdom submission.

I received a call from Apostle Hodge while I was at work. He told me that he had a special assignment for me, and he hoped I was available to help. Well, as you could imagine, here is my spiritual father requesting my assistance. The correct answer must be, "Yes, I am available!" I said to him, "If I can help, I am more than willing!"

He said, "There is a 3-day conference coming up that LPCC has been asked to support." He said, "Pastor Linda and I will be speaking, but I would like you to be a speaker for the Ministry of Helps segment." The topic for the segment was "How to Support Kingdom Vision." Apostle Hodge said, "I had other people in mind for the assignment, but I put you first on the list." I told him, I would be more than willing to speak at the event, but that I had never spoken at an event on this level." He said, "I understand, but you don't have to worry because the grace that is on me for purpose, will be on you for purpose." I said, "Ok sir, I am available!"

Antoinette (my wife) and I made plans to attend the event. The first blessing of Kingdom submission was experienced when we reserved hotel accommodations at the Westin Hotel. We secured a room for less than half the regular price. The Westin Hotel is an expensive 4-5 star hotel, but because the favor of Kingdom submission was at work in my life, the Lord ensured that my price was greatly reduced . . . PTL!

When we arrived at the event for the first day, all the speakers were requested to come early for an event briefing. When we arrived at the room the person at the door asked me my name. I said, "Sylvester Bell." The person looked at the list, but he said, "I don't see your name." I said, "I was invited by Apostle Fred Hodge." The person said, "Please enter." When we walked in the room everyone there was either an Apostle, Prophet, Bishop, or Senior Pastor. We looked for Apostle Hodge and Pastor Linda and we sat by them. Because of my connection to my spiritual father and mother, I gained entrance to a room set aside for advanced-level ministry gifts.

The first speaker at the conference was Pastor Linda. She spoke by the power of the Holy Spirit and established the expectation for the remaining speakers. Apostle Hodge was slated to speak at the main evening service. After Pastor Linda and another speaker finished their presentations, it was time for the breakout sessions. The Leadership Ministry Gifts were directed to go to another room and all Ministry of Helps workers were asked to stay in the main sanctuary. I was scheduled to speak to the Ministry of Helps workers. As Apostle

Hodge and Pastor Linda were leaving to go to their session, I became nervous. I believe the Holy Spirit knew I needed one last encouragement. Before leaving the main sanctuary, Pastor Linda looked back at me and said by the power of the Holy Spirit, "BE YOURSELF!" I responded to her and said, "Yes Ma'am!"

After my exchange of words with Pastor Linda, the grace transfer of confidence and power was activated in me. When I began to speak to the audience, the power of the Holy Spirit for ministry began to flow in my presentation. It seemed that every word and analogy fitted like a well-tailored suit. The audience was noticeably being blessed by my lesson. At the end of the session, a woman came to me and said, "That was outstanding, what is the name of your church?" I told her I was a support pastor at Living Praise Christian Church. She said, "You are not the senior pastor? If you are not the senior pastor, then who is the senior pastor?" I told her our senior pastor is Apostle Fred Hodge. "If I was blessed tremendously by your ministry, I must hear Apostle Hodge!" I told her he was speaking that evening. "I will be there!"

Antoinette and I left the first day of the conference, giving praise, thanks, and glory to God for His blessing and favor for ministry. It is obvious that because of my connection to God and my spiritual father, the power of Kingdom submission was active in my life.

Praise break: Glory to God!

PRAYER

Father God, my relationship with You is contingent on me submitting my life to You. Please give me a desire to build a godly relationship with You by love and Kingdom revelation. I choose to live my life to do Your will in the earth. I declare You are my God and my Lord. I make You the priority in my life. I surrender my will to Your purpose, and I ask for Your help to live a life that brings You glory. I ask for all these things in Jesus name. Amen!

CHAPTER THREE
The Power of Submission

We have come to understand that submission in the Kingdom of God is a priority for the believer. Submitting to God and His leadership brings blessings and benefits that will increase your life.

In this chapter, I want to expound on the power and benefits of having a heart of submission. For us to fully embrace the Kingdom requirement of choosing to walk in submission, we must drill deeper to gain further understanding. Earlier in the book, we concluded that submitting to God and His leadership was a wise choice. I believe after reading Chapter Three you will be further convinced that a heart of submission is the order of the day.

THE LAW OF LIFT

One worldly, misguided way of thinking about promotion and success is that those who push their way through life, without regard to the submission principle, will achieve status and personal success.

It is good to be strong-willed and have an aggressive mentality, but God has designed the social structure for mankind to live within the submission to authority organizational structure. Those who push their way past God's organized system may have some measure of perceived success, but the number one violation of this way of living is, that it puts you in opposition to God Himself. The Bible declares that the principle of submitting to authority comes from God.

> *Let every soul be subject unto the higher powers. For there is no power but of God: the powers that be are ordained of God. Whosoever, therefore,*

> *resisteth the power, resisteth the ordinance of God:*
> *and they that resist shall receive to themselves damnation.*
> Romans 13:1-2 kjv

The greatest opposition that you will ever face in life, is when you willfully choose to walk in disobedience to God's Word. God declares in His Word, *My people perish because of the lack of knowledge and the rejection of knowledge.* (Hosea 4:6) Resistance to the submission principle relegates you to a life of great limitations. Condemnation will leave you vulnerable to the attack of Satan and his cohorts. Anything that God ordains, He backs up with Kingdom authority and power.

The scripture declares that if we submit ourselves to God through humility, we will experience in our life advancement, acceleration, and ascension.

> *Humble yourselves therefore under the mighty hand of God,*
> *that he may exalt you in due time.*
> 1 Peter 5:6 kjv

What is humility? Humility is not seeing yourself as an inferior being. It is not de-voiding yourself of value, respect, and honor. The Bible says that we were fearfully and wonderfully made (see Psalm 139:14). The word "fearfully" means to be respected and the word "wonderfully" means to be honored and admired.

Humility (def):

1. To not be motivated by pride or arrogance
2. To be courteous and respectful to others
3. To submit who you are and what you have to a person or organization for a purpose

In essence, humility is a positive attitude and a way of thinking that demonstrates itself in our actions. To be humble is not weakness, but it is strength submitted for a purpose and time.

The biblical system for natural and spiritual advancement contradicts the world's system. God's system commands that you first go down before you become eligible to go up. An attitude of humility helps you assume the correct posture before God and those in leadership. The demonstration of humility identifies you as a candidate for promotion. The Bible says, *"Humble yourself under the mighty hand of God,"* which is to say, choose to comply with God's system of Kingdom submission. Compliance with God will always lead to positive things happening in your life. One of the positive things that happen when you humble yourself to God is that it activates "the Law of Lift." The Law of Lift demands that a lesser force meets a greater force which causes the lesser force to first descend, and then in time, ascend. This principle is proven in aerodynamics; before a plane can ascend it must first descend into the force of air, which eventually causes the plane to rise and take flight. The design of the wings and the position of the plane are important factors that enable the plane to take off and fly. When we submit and humble ourselves before God and leadership, it will position our lives to become candidates for promotion and ascension.

THE RIGHT PLACE AT THE RIGHT TIME

The heart of submission releases the power of God in your life and brings with it many benefits. We have learned that the Law of Lift is activated when you submit your life to God. Another benefit of the heart of submission is positioning yourself for purpose. Being in the right place at the right time is a statement that you are ready and available to receive what God has for you. The promises of God have been made available for His children, but because some are out of position, they miss the opportunity to receive what God has for them. Every blessing that is attached to purpose has a window of opportunity. It is our responsibility to ensure that we walk in harmony with God's timing to receive what God has for us.

One of the Kingdom priorities that God revealed to me is, the need to understand Kingdom cadence. Kingdom cadence will help position you to receive the blessings of God in your life and prepare you for purpose. Kingdom cadence has a great deal to do with your ability to follow God and the godly leader placed in your life. We must learn to play follow the leader to experience the benefits of Kingdom submission.

Learn to play follow the leader!

Walking in Kingdom cadence will help with the godly call on your life. It will also help with your training and development and fulfillment of Kingdom purpose.

Why should we walk in Kingdom cadence?

a) To be a help and not a hurt to the vision
b) To be a help and not a hindrance to the vision
c) To be a help and not a hater of the vision

What is Kingdom cadence?
Let us look at both words.
Kingdom (def):

- The sovereign rulership and authority of God in the heart of mankind.
- The country or territory where the will of the King is executed.
- The manifestation where the power of the King is expressed.

We are instructed by Jesus to submit to the will of the Father God, *Your Kingdom come, your will be done, on earth as it is in heaven.* (Matthew 6:10)

Cadence (def):

- The rhythmic flow of a sequence of words, sounds, or actions.
- The submission and obedience to the heartbeat of God, His leader, and His plan.
- The established order of God to be obeyed and followed.

Jesus is our primary example of walking in Kingdom cadence.

Jesus gave them this answer: "Very truly I tell you, the Son can do nothing by himself; he can do only what he sees his Father doing, because whatever the Father does the Son also does.

JOHN 5:19 NIV

For I did not speak on my own, but the Father who sent me commanded me to say all that I have spoken.

JOHN 12:49 NIV

Jesus took the time to educate His disciples regarding the necessity of walking in Kingdom cadence. The scriptures make it known that Jesus made it a priority to only do what he saw the Father God do, and only say what He heard the Father God say. Jesus provided this example for us who are believers so, we adopt this way of living because it has the power to release the benefit of Kingdom help and supply in our lives. When we walk in accordance with the will of God, we bring joy and happiness to the heart of God, and we are released to fulfill Kingdom vision and purpose. Jesus modeled the art of Kingdom cadence and fulfilled His earthly assignment to become the Savior of the world. Because of His heart of submission, we are now able to receive the power of forgiveness and salvation in our lives. Thank God for salvation!

Practicing Kingdom cadence is so important. Paul admonished the Corinthian church to follow him as he followed Christ, *Follow my example, as I follow the example of Christ.* (1 Corinthians 11:1 NIV)

In other words, Paul was saying, "Keep up—don't break rank!" Many have broken rank by failing to follow the example that Jesus and Paul left for our lives. Submission demands that you submit to the authority and plan of the King. Throughout the Bible, we find examples of Paul demonstrating the principle of Kingdom cadence. Paul was compelled by the Holy Spirit to teach, preach and build up the people by the power of God. Paul made it a priority to work toward the completion of the will of God for his life. Looking back on his life, Paul had this testimony, *I have fought the good fight, I have finished the race, I have kept the faith.* (2 Timothy 4:7 KJV)

Walking in Kingdom cadence is not a cakewalk through the park. It demands conviction and true commitment. Paul said, "I have fought a good fight." Paul made up his mind to apply pressure to his decision to follow Christ. When you choose to follow the will of God for your life, you will be faced with opposition that will test your choice and resolve. It is easy to make a confession that will not be tested. Every choice you make to honor God will be tested. The test or trial will either be spiritual or natural. Satan hates when we choose to serve God with our lives, so he releases opposition to challenge our decision and to ultimately cause us to quit. Thanks be to God; we have the power to overcome every test and trial.

Some tests are not spiritually motivated, they are just issues that arise because of life itself. Life may throw a curve ball into our experience because of our human limitations. A list of human limitations that challenge our resolve; laziness, lack of focus, physical impairment, procrastination, losing interest, and others of like sort. We must fight to overcome every challenge that comes to disrupt our decision to execute God's will for our lives.

Paul said, "I have finished the race." The objective of every race is to finish and win. The good news about our assigned Kingdom race is that we have already been given the victory. The main objective for the believer is not to focus on winning, but to focus on finishing.

The main objective for the race is to finish.
God has already given you the victory!

This revelation brings great joy and peace to my heart because God has given us an assignment that is already loaded with the promise of winning. The promise God gives to those who walk in Kingdom cadence and submission is that every step we take toward the fulfillment of purpose will work in our favor.

And we know that in all things God works for the good of those who love him, who have been called according to his purpose.
ROMANS 8:28 KJV

The name of the game is that we win!

Paul understood this truth; therefore, he did not cease moving toward completion of his godly mission because finishing was his aim (winning was a foregone conclusion). Trusting in God and believing that He will help you, will give you the motivation to finish your assigned race in life. God has given us a set of promises to help with our goal to finish the race.

I will be with you.
Be strong and of a good courage, fear not, nor be afraid of them: for the Lord thy God, he it is that doth go with thee; he will not fail thee, nor forsake thee.
DEUTERONOMY 31:6 NIV

I will not leave you.
*And the Lord, he it is that doth go before thee;
he will be with thee, he will not fail thee, neither forsake thee:
fear not, neither be dismayed.*
DEUTERONOMY 31:8 NIV

I will help you.
*God is our refuge and strength,
a very present help in trouble.*
PSALMS 46:1 NIV

There are three things that are necessary for the believer to walk in Kingdom cadence: time, sound, and rhythm.

Time – The ability to be available to perform your God-given assignment in life

Time is the God-given currency for life on earth; how you spend it will determine your life contribution to the Kingdom of God.

HOW TO UTILIZE YOUR TIME
1. Time must be respected.
    - Time must be respected because it was set by God.
    - What you do with your time will determine if you will be a success or a failure.

- What you do with your time will determine whether it will be your friend or your enemy. Jesus used His time to do the will of His Father. Jesus told His mother, *I must be about my Father's business.* (see Luke 2:49 NIV).
2. Time must be managed.
    - You must manage how you spend your time.
    - You must manage whom you spend your time with.
3. Time must be submitted to God.
    - When your time is submitted to God, He will direct your path (or time).
    - The wisdom of God will help you become effective, efficient, and energized.

Sound – The ability to hear the voice of God for revelation, instruction, and insight

> Jesus declared, *My sheep know my voice,
> and the voice of another they will not follow.*
> JOHN 10:4-5 NKJV

God gave us an ear to hear His voice. The ear is comprised of two components:

1. The outer-ear to locate sound – To determine the credibility of the source.
2. The inner ear to receive sound – To judge whether it complies with the voice of God and the voice of the leader.

On the way to the Promised Land, the children of Israel listened to the wrong voice (sound) and some of them missed their purpose and destiny.

Rhythm – The ability to walk in harmony with God, His leader, and the vision requires a heart of submission and obedience.

The scripture tells us if we are willing and obedient, we will have success in life (see Isaiah 1:19).

David walked in Kingdom cadence and fulfilled his purpose and destiny. He had a heart submitted to God.

> *And when he had removed him, he raised up unto them*
> *David to be their king; to whom also he gave testimony, and said,*
> *I have found David the son of Jesse, a man after mine own heart,*
> *which shall fulfil all my will.*
>
> Acts 13:22 kjv

David's father devalued him, his brothers discounted him, Goliath dishonored him but none of them could stop him because he kept good Kingdom Cadence.

When you walk in Kingdom cadence, God places a special blessing on your life called the anointing. The anointing has the power to help you accomplish God's will and complete the purpose and destiny for your life.

WHAT IS THE ANOINTING?

Anointing (def):
- The anointing is the release of God's approval and power on people, places, and things for Kingdom purpose.
- The anointing is the endowment of God's power for function. We are anointed to do something.

God revealed to man His intent to assign His Spirit upon man for His Kingdom purpose.

> *And it shall come to pass afterward, that I will pour out my*
> *spirit upon all flesh; and your sons and your daughters*
> *shall prophesy, your old men shall dream dreams,*
> *your young men shall see visions: And also upon the servants and upon*
> *the handmaids in those days will I pour out my spirit.*
> JOEL 2:28-29 KJV

The anointing is given to those who are appointed. Those who are appointed will be anointed. Find your purpose in God and you will tap into your place of anointing. The anointing will make you effective and you will produce Kingdom results. The difference between David and his brothers was that David was appointed by God for the assignment to be King of Israel. When you read the story about David and his selection, it appears that God makes the wrong choice in appointing him. One of his brothers seemed to be a better candidate for the assignment. There is one immutable fact in the Kingdom of God, God Himself reserves the right to choose whomsoever He will (see Psalm 75:7). One of the limitations of man is that we depend on our natural abilities (intellect, knowledge, and experience) to make decisions in life. When God selects you for a task, expect that godly instructions and power will be forthcoming. David is selected to be king, but his success in accomplishing the will of God is highly contingent upon him walking in Kingdom cadence (godly rhythm) with God's plan and purpose. David is challenged spiritually and naturally when he accepts the call of God. He is equipped for the challenge because of the anointing.

HEART OF SUBMISSION

DAVID ANOINTED TO BE KING

Now the LORD said to Samuel, "You have mourned long enough for Saul. I have rejected him as king of Israel, so fill your flask with olive oil and go to Bethlehem. Find a man named Jesse who lives there, for I have selected one of his sons to be my king.

1 SAMUEL 16:1 NLT

In the same way, all seven of Jesse's sons were presented to Samuel. But Samuel said to Jesse, "The LORD has not chosen any of these." Then Samuel asked, "Are these all the sons you have?" "There is still the youngest," Jesse replied. "But he's out in the fields watching the sheep and goats." "Send for him at once," Samuel said. "We will not sit down to eat until he arrives." So Jesse sent for him. He was dark and handsome, with beautiful eyes. And the LORD said, "This is the one; anoint him." So as David stood there among his brothers, Samuel took the flask of olive oil he had brought and anointed David with the oil. And the Spirit of the LORD came powerfully upon David from that day on. Then Samuel returned to Ramah.

1 SAMUEL 16:10-13 NLT

FACTS ABOUT THE ANOINTING

1. The anointing signifies you are chosen by God (see 2 Kings 9:6). God anoints those He appoints.
2. The anointing will find you even when others try to keep you down. Jesse neglected to bring David before Saul because he considered David to be unworthy and unqualified to become the King of Israel.

3. The anointing will not stay hidden or concealed. Moses's mother hid him until she could no longer keep him hidden because of the anointing (see Exodus 2:3).
4. The anointing will bring those who are faithful from the back to the front. David was assigned to the backside of the mountain with a few sheep but moved to the front after he was appointed and anointed by God.
5. The anointing will equip you for a good fight with the enemy. David was sent to bring food to his brothers who were at war. Because David did not refuse what seemed to be a menial task, his lower-level obedience brought him to his higher-level purpose, which was to fight Goliath (see I Samuel 17:17-23).

Lower-Level Obedience Leads to Higher Level Purpose – Obey God!

6. The anointing will increase your understanding and wisdom and cause you to operate on high levels (see Isaiah 11:2).
7. The anointing is fueled by a life of praise and worship to God. David became an expert at ushering in the presence of the Lord (see 2 Samuel 6:14-15).

Because David was submitted to God, he experienced the blessing of being in the right place at the right time. We can learn much from those who took advantage of this principle, to ensure that our lives are enhanced and positioned for success.

PRAYER

Father God, walking in harmony with Your will for my life is a priority. You created me with purpose, for purpose, on purpose. Walking in

Kingdom cadence ensures that I am available for Your will to be done in my life. Lord, I ask that the Holy Spirit lead and guide me, so I remain in lockstep with You, Your will, and Your way. I submit to Your direction and correction which helps to keep me safe and available for your purpose in my life. Lord, I allow the principles of time, sound, and rhythm to help me remain in the bosom of Your will. I understand that a heart of submission requires that I follow You completely so that I will be a support to the Kingdom. Thank You for Your guidance in Jesus name. Amen!

CHAPTER FOUR
A Man After God's Own Heart

One of the realities of life we must come to understand, is that God reserves the right to have things the way He wants. God is the Creator of all things; therefore, He receives the right to raise one up and tear one down. He has the right to choose who will represent Him on the earth. God is particular; therefore, He seeks a candidate to represent Him in the earth that has His heart in mind.

What does it mean to be a man after God's own heart? A man after God's own heart means the following:

a) You must love God with all your heart, soul, and body.
b) You must be willing to submit your life to God and His will.
c) You must walk in harmony with God. What is important to Him must be important to you.

Connection to God, and knowledge about God, are essential for you to begin your path in developing a heart after God. Many have tried to serve God from the neck up, but they have failed miserably because God requires us to give our whole selves to abide with Him.

Let us take the time to get to know God and what pleases Him.

THE HEART OF GOD

For a relationship to function properly, there must be an understanding of what is expected from all individuals involved in the relationship. The most important relationship we must pursue is a relationship with God. It is one thing to know about Him, but it is another thing to know Him. Jesus said in His Word that we must make it a priority to know and submit to God.

> *But seek ye first the kingdom of God, and his righteousness,*
> *and all these things shall be added unto you.*
> MATTHEW 6:33 KJV

The word *seek* means to pursue, follow, go after, or run after. The first step in seeking God is giving your life to Him by accepting Jesus as Savior and Lord. It is futile to think that you can connect to God any other way. Jesus is the door to relationship and fellowship with the Father God (see John 10:9). Why are we rejected by God in certain endeavors? Could it be that we are out of His will and His way? God will not force us to follow His will, but He reserves the right to withhold His presence and provision if we violate His will for our lives. Many have failed in life and suffered dire consequences because of rebellion and disobedience to God's will. The scripture teaches us that rebellion and disobedience are a direct violation of God's will.

> *For rebellion is as the sin of witchcraft and stubbornness is as iniquity*
> *and idolatry. Because thou hast rejected the word of the Lord,*
> *he hath also rejected thee from being king.*
> 1 SAMUEL 15:23 KJV

In the scripture, we see that rebellion and stubbornness (disobedience) will cause God to reject us. Rebellion says that I submit and trust in someone or something other than God. Disobedience says I choose to ignore the will of God and make myself the focus of attention. Both violations are manifested when we fail to submit our lives to God and follow His will and way. Satan is our ultra-example of this egregious violation. He openly rebelled against the will of God and suffered the ultimate judgment of rejection.

We learned earlier in the book, that many times we fail in life because of the lack of knowledge or the rejection of knowledge. God is eager to have a relationship with His creation, but it must be on His terms. If we are to pursue a relationship with God, we must know His heart and what pleases Him.

Well, enough build-up for this important Kingdom fact. What is the heart of God or what pleases God? The heart of God is obedience. When you learn and practice this immutable Kingdom principle, it will enrich and deepen your relationship with God. God told Samuel, "I am looking for a man to be King of Israel who has my heart."

Obedience is What Moves God!

Connecting to God and obtaining His favor is connected to your obedience to His will. Saul was chosen to be the king of Israel, but he lacked a heart of submission which is an important component necessary for Kingdom purpose. Saul looked and sounded like a king, but his qualities emanated from a place of pride.

Saul's Decline Because of Disobedience

Saul's pride robbed him of the revelation of how to please God. Truth be told, Saul's desire to please himself outweighed his desire to please God. Whenever we put anything or anyone above the will of God, we have entered a place of decline and destruction.

The initial sign of Saul's decline happened when preparing for a battle with the Philistines. The Philistines had gathered a large army to fight the Israelites. Samuel directed Saul to wait for him to offer a burnt offering to

God for the Lord's help in the battle. Samuel did not show up in a timely manner, so Saul offered the burnt offering on his own accord. This was a violation of godly protocol because Samuel was authorized by God to conduct the burnt offering, not Saul. Saul's actions were provoked by fear and pride.

> *And some of the Hebrews went over Jordan to the land of Gad and Gilead. As for Saul, he was yet in Gilgal, and all the people followed him trembling. And he tarried seven days, according to the set time that Samuel had appointed: but Samuel came not to Gilgal; and the people were scattered from him. And Saul said, Bring hither a burnt offering to me, and peace offerings. And he offered the burnt offering. And it came to pass, that as soon as he had made an end of offering the burnt offering, behold, Samuel came; and Saul went out to meet him, that he might salute him. And Samuel said, What hast thou done?*
> *And Saul said, Because I saw that the people were scattered from me, and that thou camest not within the days appointed, and that the Philistines gathered themselves together at Michmash;*
> *Therefore said I, The Philistines will come down now upon me to Gilgal, and I have not made supplication unto the Lord: I forced myself, therefore, and offered a burnt offering. And Samuel said to Saul, Thou hast done foolishly: thou hast not kept the commandment of the Lord thy God, which he commanded thee: for now would the Lord have established thy kingdom upon Israel forever. But now thy kingdom shall not continue: the Lord hath sought him a man after his own heart, and the Lord hath commanded him to be captain over his people, because thou hast not kept that which the Lord commanded thee.*
> 1 SAMUEL 13:7-14 KJV

This story provides us a clear example of disobedience and the consequences that come with the choice to disobey God. We must learn that God requires us to maintain obedience even in the face of adversity. I could only imagine how Saul felt seeing his men begin to lose heart because things did not go as expected, but it is the leader's responsibility to showcase and inspire obedience in tough times. Saul's display of disobedience revealed that he put his trust in man rather than God; remember rebellion is trusting someone other than God. Saul should have waited for Samuel to arrive and strongly encouraged the men to follow his example of obedience. Saul's actions provoked the wrath and judgment of God. Saul missed the opportunity for His lineage to experience the call and blessing of God for Kingdom leadership. Disobedience not only impacts your life but also impacts the lives of those in your lineage.

We should not be so judgmental of Saul because many of us fail to follow Kingdom protocol day after day. It is easy to walk in disobedience because it usually involves an act of convenience. The challenge of being obedient requires three things: courage, faith, and trust in God. Our resolve to walk in obedience will usually be tested by Satan or humanity. Satan has a valued interest in you choosing to disobey God because he knows if you follow the will of God, you will succeed in life. We were created with the right to choose our own path in life; therefore, Satan's strategy is to get you to follow His will for your life or your own path with your limited understanding.

Either way, Satan knows you are destined to fail if you do not follow the will of God for your life. Therefore, we must develop a heart of submission to God to give Him the right to bless our lives with His presence and power. We are directed by the Word of God to trust in God with obedience.

HEART OF SUBMISSION

Trust in the Lord with all thine heart and lean not unto thine own understanding. In all thy ways acknowledge him, and he shall direct thy paths.

PROVERBS 3:5-6 KJV

The evidence that we trust God is displayed when we obey God.

Saul had another recorded incident where he grossly violated the will of God. Saul was directed to rid Israel of a generational enemy that would plague God's people for a long time. Saul was commanded by Samuel for the army of Israel to totally wipe out the Amalekites. It was the will of God.

Samuel said to Saul, "I am the one the Lord sent to anoint you king over his people Israel; so listen now to the message from the Lord. This is what the Lord Almighty says: 'I will punish the Amalekites for what they did to Israel when they waylaid them as they came up from Egypt. Now go, attack the Amalekites and totally destroy all that belongs to them. Do not spare them; put to death men and women, children and infants, cattle and sheep, camels and donkeys.'"

SAMUEL 15:1-3 KJV

The Amalekites and their king, Agag, represented opposition to the success of the Israel nation living a godly lifestyle and establishing God's Kingdom on the earth. The Amalekites were a mortal enemy who, time after time, opposed God's people and joined other nations who had the same objective, to destroy Israel.

As we read the story regarding the battle with the Amalekites, we see that Saul had no problem killing Amalekite men, women, children, and livestock. Saul chose to spare King Agag and the best of the Amalekite livestock.

> *But Saul and the army spared Agag and the best of the sheep and cattle, the fat calves and lambs-everything that was good. These they were unwilling to destroy completely, but everything that was despised and weak they totally destroyed.*
> 1 Samuel 15:9 kjv

Saul's actions totally displeased God which expedited Saul's demotion. God made known his rejection of Saul as king and set the wheels in motion for Saul to be removed "henceforth." God will not tolerate disobedience from those in leadership, who seek to do things their own way. God sees disobedience from leaders as "great sin." Great sin is judged on the highest levels. "To whom much is given, much is required."

Saul lost his way and his position because he did not have a heart after God. God demands for those who serve Him to be totally submitted to His will and way. We must not allow pride, fear, or intimidation from others to move us to disobedience, because it will ultimately become our demise.

The Kingdom of God is never stagnant; therefore, God employed the concept of next man up. God found another man who did have a heart after God. God had to go to the fields to find a shepherd who was a prime candidate for the open position.

David's Ascension Because of Obedience

God sent Samuel on a search to locate the next King of Israel.

> *The Lord said to Samuel, "How long will you mourn for Saul since I have rejected him as king over Israel? Fill your horn with oil and be on your way; I am sending you to Jesse of Bethlehem. I have chosen one of his sons to be king." But Samuel said, "How can I go? If Saul hears*

*about it, he will kill me." The Lord said, "Take a heifer with you
and say, I have come to sacrifice to the Lord."*

SAMUEL 16:1-2 KJV

Samuel began his search for the next king of Israel, but you know it was with mixed emotions because he loved Saul. Samuel demonstrates for us an especially important principle, we must be willing to obey God even when it causes emotional discomfort.

Samuel had to overcome another challenge to obeying God—if Saul discovered that Samuel was looking for his replacement, he would kill Samuel. Samuel had to employ trust and faith in God's protection.

Sometimes, doing the will of God is not an easy task. We must fight the good fight of faith to successfully follow God's will. We will be faced with challenges in life that will seek to discourage us from our conviction and commitment.

Samuel finds David in the house of Jesse, but not without a challenge. Samuel arrives to Bethlehem to find the next king of Israel, but he employs a strategy that limits his godly sight and discernment.

And Samuel did that which the Lord spake and came to Bethlehem. And the elders of the town trembled at his coming, and said, Comest thou peaceably? And he said, Peaceably: I am come to sacrifice unto the Lord: sanctify yourselves, and come with me to the sacrifice. And he sanctified Jesse and his sons, and called them to the sacrifice.
And it came to pass, when they were come, that he looked on Eliab, and said, Surely the Lord's anointed is before him. But the Lord said unto Samuel, Look not on his countenance, or on the height of his stature; because I have refused him: for the Lord seeth not as man seeth; for man looketh on the outward appearance, but the Lord looketh on the heart. Then Jesse called Abinadab, and made him pass before Samuel. And he

said Neither hath the Lord chosen this. Then Jesse made Shammah to pass by. And he said Neither hath the Lord chosen this. Again, Jesse made seven of his sons to pass before Samuel. And Samuel said unto Jesse, The Lord hath not chosen these.
                                                    1 Samuel 16:4-10 kjv

Based on physical description and sensibility, one of David's brothers seemed more suitable candidate for the next King of Israel. Samuel was surprised that none of David's brothers met God's requirements. God gave Samuel a piece of revelation that helped him understand God's selection process. God informed Samuel that man looks on the outer man, but God looks at the heart. Man looks at your physical attributes, but God looks for a godly heart of submission! Samuel could have anointed one of David's brothers, but he would just have had another Saul.

When choosing someone to be a Kingdom leader, God will look at what is in their heart. Those who live by their flesh display attributes that are self-pleasing and self-seeking. Those who live by the spirit display attributes that are centered around pleasing God and doing His will. Your priority in life must always be God first.

Samuel may not have known exactly who God had selected to be the next King of Israel, but he did know who God had not selected. Samuel was an experienced prophet; therefore, God would not send him on a wasted trip. He asked Jesse, "Do you have another son not present?" Jesse is forced to mention his son of dishonor and perceived deceit.

And Samuel said unto Jesse, Are here all thy children? And he said, There remaineth yet the youngest, and, behold, he keepeth the sheep. And Samuel said unto Jesse, Send and fetch him: for we will not sit down till he come hither. And he sent, and brought him in. Now he was ruddy, and withal of a beautiful countenance, and goodly to look to.

*And the Lord said, Arise, anoint him: for this is he. Then Samuel took
the horn of oil, and anointed him in the midst of his brethren:
and the Spirit of the Lord came upon David from that day forward.
So Samuel rose up, and went to Ramah.*

SAMUEL 16:11-13 KJV

Wow! It is great to know that if you are selected by God, no one or nothing can keep you from your destiny! When Samuel sees David, God makes it known that David is God's choice for the next King of Israel. Apparently, David was filled with the stuff godly kings are made of. Samuel anoints David in front of his father, brothers, and those who were watching. God is deliberate and He does not leave room for misunderstanding, God directs Samuel to anoint David so all can see. The anointing brings with it the Spirit of the Lord for grace and power to execute purpose. The Bible records various exploits of David and his ability to please God. David was not perfect in any manner, but he had a genuine heart to please God. It also helped that David was a worshipper. David's life displayed his love and reverence for God.

Worship and praise will escort you into the presence of God where there is peace, joy, and blessing for purpose. Those who have learned the art of worship and service to God, make themselves viable candidates for Kingdom purpose. The heart of God requires obedience! When we connect to God by worship, God's Spirit joins with our spirit and gives us a supernatural boost to be who He says we are, to do what He says we can do, to have what He says we can have.

THE WILL OF GOD

An important piece to pleasing God and having success in life is doing things God's way. Doing things God's way is called righteous living. What does the phrase "the will of God" mean? The will of God is the plan and desire of God for heaven and earth. As the creator and engineer of all things, God knows and has established instructions for Kingdom living. Jesus gave us explicit instructions for our daily focus. Jesus told the disciples to include in their prayer focus, *Your kingdom come. You will be done in earth as it is in heaven.* (Matthew 6:10) Jesus was speaking of the will of God being fulfilled in the earth like it is already being done in heaven. Isaiah received a vision of God sitting on His throne in heaven and saw the angels worshipping and serving God.

> *In the year that King Uzziah died, I saw the Lord sitting on a throne, high and lifted up, and the train of His robe filled the temple. Above it stood seraphim; each one had six wings: with two he covered his face, with two he covered his feet, and with two he flew. And one cried to another and said: "Holy, holy, holy is the Lord of hosts; The whole earth is full of His glory!"*
> ISAIAH 6:1-3 KJV

In Isaiah's vision, God is sitting on His throne of authority and the angels are worshipping and serving God. The angels have six wings:

Two wings cover their face – representing reverence and deep respect for God

Two wings cover their feet – representing their willingness to serve God

Two wings to fly – representing the haste in which the will of God is done

Like the angels, we must have a deep reverence for God and be quick to serve God with our lives. A life submitted to God is a life that brings glory to God. The highest call we can ever receive is, to do the will of God in the earth. When we do the will of God, we openly witness His authority, ability, and power in the earth. Picture this, God took a holy man who became unholy by sin, then God put His Holy Spirit in man by salvation, and then put the man back in an unholy world and caused him to live holy. Wow, what a demonstration of power! Even though we may start out in life with unholy lives, God has the power to transform us into agents of holiness with His Holy Spirit. When you have the Holy Spirit on the inside, you have the power to do the will of God.

Jesus made it His life's goal to do the will of the Father in word and deed.

> *For I have not spoken of myself; but the Father which sent me, he gave me a commandment, what I should say, and what I should speak.*
> JOHN 12:49 KJV

> *Then answered Jesus and said unto them, Verily, verily, I say unto you, The Son can do nothing of himself, but what he seeth the Father do: for what things soever he doeth, these also doeth the Son likewise.*
> JOHN 5:19 KJV

What we say and do must align with the will of God for our lives. What you say about your life will become law for you. If you say I am a winner, you will become a winner. If you say I am a loser, you will become a loser. God gave man the power of choice to choose to do things his own way or to follow the ordained godly plan for his life. If we choose to follow God's plan for our lives, what God has predestined will become a reality.

What we say and do must align with the will of God. This is the very expression of submission that speaks of God's authority in heaven and earth. We are speaking spirits; therefore, we must use our words to provide marching orders for our lives. God created man and gave him the power of choice to decide the direction for his life. God will not force His will on man, but he will beckon man to submit, to His will. When man submits his life to God, the life that God has predestined for him becomes possible.

How do we discover the will of God for our lives? God has left His instructions for our lives in His Word. The Word of God is the primary source of direction for godly living.

For I am not ashamed of the gospel of Christ:
for it is the power of God unto salvation to every one that believeth;
to the Jew first, and also to the Greek.

ROMAN 1:16 KJV

THE WORD OF GOD FOR LIVING

It is the Word of God (the logos) that is filled with doctrine, revelation, and information that will reveal the will of God to man. We are requested to study God's Word to gain the revelation and teaching regarding God's will.

Study to shew thyself approved unto God, a workman that needeth not to be ashamed, rightly dividing the word of truth.

2 TIMOTHY 2:15

The study and reading of God's Word will provide vital information for the believer's expected lifestyle. Remember, we are cautioned in the Word of God that if we fail to obtain the knowledge of God's Word, we will perish (become naked, ignorant, destined to fail).

THE HOLY SPIRIT IS OUR GUIDE

The Word of God provides the instructions necessary for the believer's lifestyle. God understood for man to be able to live what was written, he was going to need supernatural help. Before Jesus left the earth, He told the disciples, "I will not leave you comfortless or without help, I will send you heavenly support." Jesus sent the Holy Spirit to be our Help with Kingdom living.

> *Howbeit when he, the Spirit of truth, is come, he will guide you into all truth: for he shall not speak of himself; but whatsoever he shall hear, that shall he speak: and he will shew you things to come. He shall glorify me: for he shall receive of mine, and shall shew it unto you.*
>
> JOHN 16:13-14 KJV

The Holy Spirit has been assigned to provide the help man needs to do the will of God. The Word gives instructions, but the Holy Spirit gives us the power to follow the Word. It takes more than a desire to do God's will. We need the power of God to overcome the challenges that block our efforts. Satan and his cohorts will not just stand by while you purpose to live for God. Thanks be to God for providing the spiritual help we need to overcome the enemy! We also must contend with our flesh (sinful nature), to overcome the ungodly desires that war against us fulfilling God's will for our lives. The Holy Spirit understands our predicament; therefore, He works with us to provide the support necessary to live by the will of God. The Holy Spirit is the third person of the Trinity, so he helped to create man and He knows the path set for mankind. He also has a direct link to the Father and the Son to discuss action planning for your life.

Following the directions of The Holy Spirit, is like following the directions of a GPS to get to a desired location. When we place a desired destination in the GPS and press start, the GPS will provide the most efficient directions to your desired location. If you follow the directions of the GPS, you will arrive at your location. The Holy Spirit is our heavenly GPS for life. When we set our life course according to the will of God, and press start by prayer, the Holy Spirit will provide directions and support to get us to our godly destination.

One of the provisions of the Holy Spirit is that He will help us even when we get off track. Just like the GPS, when we get off the track of our designed route, the Holy Spirit will provide directions to help us get to our desired destination. The GPS will not yell or belittle you but will let you know you are off track and indicate "recalculating" to get you back on track to your destination. The Holy Spirit is a gentleman. Just like GPS, He will notify you when you are off the track of purpose and destiny and recalculate directions to get you back on track in fulfilling God's will for your life.

TESTIFY

When I was 16 years old, I gave my life to Christ. The Lord put in my heart a desire to become a minister of God's Word in the earth. I began to develop myself by studying God's Word and establishing a necessary prayer life. I received the baptism of the Holy Spirit, which provided the spiritual support needed to live a spiritual lifestyle. As long as I followed the Word of God and relied on the Holy Spirit to direct my life, I continued to walk in divine purpose.

I got married at an early age and encountered some life challenges that caused me and my wife to divorce. Because I did not follow God's Word and did not listen to the Holy Spirit, I broke my relationship with God. For ten years I lived a backslidden lifestyle. I was so unhappy and desired to regain my relationship with God. Even though I had rejected God, He did not cease to reconnect with me. Eventually, I remarried, and my wife (Antoinette Bell) began to pray for my restoration with God. I am happy to say that I rededicated my life to God and my relationship with Him was restored! I thought because I fell away from God, that my original call to be a minister of the gospel was forfeited. The Holy Spirit arranged for me to connect with Apostle Fred Hodge, Jr., and he met with me to discuss my life and call. He informed me that my life with God was repairable

and that my call was still intact. He placed me on a restoration plan to help reestablish my spiritual strength. I am so pleased to say, that not only was my relationship with God restored but I was also put back on track for the fulfillment of God's call on my life. Thanks to God for not forgetting me and welcoming me back with open arms! The Holy Spirit, like the GPS, set a course for me to fulfill the call on my life!

PRAISE BREAK!!!

THE WAY OF GOD

God is a peculiar Being. He does not operate in a conventional manner. It may seem that God would use conventional means to execute His will, but like Frank Sinatra once sang, God does things His way. God does not seek to do right; what God does is right. The ways of God are not based on insensibility and logic, the ways of God are based on His will. The ways of God are a sight to behold, as we will learn in this chapter.

There are countless examples of the ways of God in the Bible. They give a clear indication that God believes in working outside the box. In my years on this earth, I have marveled at the ways of God and His uncanny ability to get things done His way. Well, it would be reasonable to assume that if you are the Creator of all things, you have the right to impose your will and way whenever you desire.

First, let us establish an immutable truth, God's ways are totally different from the ways of man.

> *Seek ye the Lord while he may be found, call ye upon him while he is near: Let the wicked forsake his way, and the unrighteous man his thoughts: and let him return unto the Lord, and he will have mercy upon him; and to our God, for he will abundantly pardon. For my thoughts are not your thoughts, neither are your ways my ways, saith the Lord. For as the heavens are higher than the earth, so are my ways higher than your ways, and my thoughts than your thoughts.*
>
> Isaiah 55:6-9 KJV

The scriptures give us a clear indication that the ways of God are different from our ways. The ways of God speak to the way He will manifest His will and get things done in heaven and earth. As we see in the scripture, the way of God is supported by His thoughts. The thoughts of God come from a pure source of holiness and righteousness that give Him the ability to create a strategy for His purposes. We are commanded to forsake (or abandon) our thoughts and ways to receive a godly download regarding Kingdom strategy. When you submit to the ways of God, you will realize greater pathway and modus operandi for Kingdom success.

The Bible tells us to acknowledge God in all our ways when making decisions for our lives, *In all thy ways acknowledge him, and he shall direct thy paths.* (Proverbs 3:6) To acknowledge God means to submit to His will and ways concerning your life and decisions. When we acknowledge God, we are saying, "Your ways are higher (better) than our ways!" God will not impose Himself into your life, but He will respond to your request for help. When God comes into your situation, He brings His unlimited resources to help you walk in success.

God's ways are supported by His righteousness, truth, wisdom, and power. God's righteousness is fueled by a pure source of holiness. The righteousness of God is God's way of doing things. Many say that God cannot violate His will, but I say that God will not violate His will because it is His chosen way to operate in heaven and in earth. God has an unfair advantage because He is the Creator of truth and He lives by the truth He has created. The Bible says that truth will make and set us free (see John 8:32). The truth of God's Word reveals His way for our lives both spiritually and naturally. The wisdom of God is the mind of God one what you should do. Wisdom is different from knowledge. Knowledge is knowing what to do, but wisdom is knowing when to do what you know. The wisdom of God introduces an element of expedience for our situations. The Bible says, in the book of Ecclesiastes, that there is a time for various situations and knowing how to conduct yourself in every season of time, comes by the wisdom of God. The way of God is also supported by the power of God. What good is having righteousness, truth, and wisdom if you do not have power to back it up? The power of God is without question, a defining source of strength that enables God to enforce His will and way.

The ways of God bring glory to His name. God loves using people, places, and things that give Him the best opportunity to showcase His power and bring glory to His name.

*But God hath chosen the foolish things of the world to confound
the wise, and God hath chosen the weak things of the
world to confound the things which are mighty;*
1 Corinthians 1:27 kjv

God selected David to be king of Israel because it was obvious that David would not be a premier choice in the eyes of man. David was young and the least in his father's house.

Then Samuel asked, "Are these all the sons you have?" "There is still the youngest," Jesse replied. "But he's out in the fields watching the sheep and goats." "Send for him at once," Samuel said. "We will not sit down to eat until he arrives." So Jesse sent for him. He was dark and handsome, with beautiful eyes. And the Lord said, "This is the one; anoint him."
1 Samuel 16:11-12 nlt

David's selection to be the king of Israel did not seem to make sense, but it did afford God an opportunity to use the situation to make a statement of His wisdom and power. David's first kingly assignment to fight Goliath, was an opportunity for God to put His plan into action. Goliath was a man of war.

*Then Goliath, a Philistine champion from Gath, came out of the
Philistine ranks to face the forces of Israel. He was over nine feet tall! He
wore a bronze helmet, and his bronze coat of mail weighed 125 pounds.
He also wore bronze leg armor, and he carried a bronze javelin on his
shoulder. The shaft of his spear was as heavy and thick as a weaver's
beam, tipped with an iron spearhead that weighed 15 pounds.
His armor bearer walked ahead of him carrying a shield.*
1 Samuel 17:4-7 nlt

The eye test would reveal that the Goliath vs. David UFC match fight would be an unfair match. The thing that the Philistines did not realize is that David had an unfair advantage—the Lord was with David!

> *David replied to the Philistine, "You come to me with sword, spear, and javelin, but I come to you in the name of the Lord of Heaven's Armies-the God of the armies of Israel, whom you have defied."*
> 1 SAMUEL 17:45 NLT

God took the opportunity to use David to make a powerful statement of His wisdom, power, and might. We all know the story—David uses a slingshot and a rock to defeat Goliath. The reason why David was able to defeat Goliath with meager weapons was because by themselves, the slingshot and rock are ordinary and limited, but with God's help, the slingshot and rock become supernatural weapons. David was submitted to God and anointed by God; therefore, anything that he touched or used would also be anointed by God. Believers must be submitted to God and like David, we will be anointed by God to overcome insurmountable odds.

The ways of God sometimes do not seem to make sense, but they are filled with Kingdom power to bring glory to God and cause the believer to walk in a life of success.

PRAYER

Father God, it is my desire to make Your priority in my life. I love You with all my heart, soul, and body. Please help me to develop a heart that is aggressively after Your will and way. David was a man after Your own heart, this is the testimony that I want to live and leave in the earth. I submit myself to the Holy Spirit for leadership and guidance. Please use my heart, my hands, and my feet to accomplish Your will and Your way. All these things I ask in Jesus name. Amen!

CHAPTER FIVE
The Set Man

God is the creator of heaven and earth. Therefore, it is His expectation that both be submitted to His rulership. The Bible declares that God has complete control in heaven. God is totally responsible for ruling and reigning in heaven, but God has given man delegated authority for ruling and reigning in the earth. *The heaven, even the heavens, are the Lord's: but the earth hath he given to the children of men.* (Psalm 115:16) Man has been given the privilege to rule and reign in the earth. The privilege of ruling and reigning in the earth brings great responsibility and accountability. The opportunity to be a leader is an honor and privilege, but it also brings great responsibility. The responsibility of leadership should compel you to seek God for wisdom and knowledge so that you can be a good leader.

Because of God's decree regarding earthy rulership, it is God's will and way to choose men and women who have His approval to represent Him in the earth. Those chosen by God for this level of leadership are called the "Set Man." The Set Man is responsible for maintaining a strong relationship with God and hearing from God to obtain the vision for Kingdom purpose and leadership.

> *I will stand my watch and set myself on the rampart, And watch to see what He will say to me, And what I will answer when I am corrected. Then the Lord answered me and said: "Write the vision and make it plain on tablets, That he may run who reads it. For the vision is yet for an appointed time, But at the end, it will speak, and it will not lie. Though it tarries, wait for it; Because it will surely come, It will not tarry."*
>
> HABAKKUK 2:1-3 KJV

We are told in scripture that the vision must be received from God and documented for guidance and dissemination to others. God does not give the vision to many. He gives it to one to be shared with others. This is an excellent strategy because it eliminates the opportunity for confusion. The concept of one mouth to one ear helps to greatly reduce misunderstanding. Moses was called to be a set man. God made it known that to Moses, *I speak face to face and to others I speak to in vision and dream."* (see Numbers 12:6-8). The Set Man has God's full attention when receiving direction for Kingdom purpose.

God will not intrude in the affairs of man unless His help is requested. We have the privilege to go to the Throne of Grace and request God's help when we need it (see Hebrews 4:16). A sign of true leadership and wisdom is to first seek the Lord for help in our situations. When God enters the affairs of man by request, He enters the situation with superior support. God brings to the situation His presence and power. When God is present, His omnipresence is available. That means God will be ever-present support in your situation. When God is present, His omniscient knowledge and revelation are present. That means God's unlimited knowledge and revelation are present in your situation. When God is present, his omnipotence is available. That means God's supernatural power is present in your situation. When you have God's support, you have what is needed to encounter any situation or difficulty.

CHOSEN BY GOD

The Bible declares, *"Many are called but few are chosen."* Why are the few chosen? Because they said "yes" to the call. God loves when men and women say yes to the call of service in the Kingdom. One important fact that you should know is that God does not necessarily choose "yes men." God is not looking for "yes men," but He is looking for men who will say yes to the call! What is the difference between "yes men" and men who will say yes? "Yes men," say yes without deliberation; therefore, their yes, will not carry the weight of their commitment. A man, who will say yes, will take time to consider and deliberate their decision to say yes. This person will take the time to consider the weight of their decision. Their commitment to say yes is supported by commitment and loyalty.

God chose Moses to be a deliverer for the Children of Israel. Before Moses said yes to the call of God, he had a set of questions. God wanted Moses to say yes to the call, but God did not discount Moses for inquiring about his assignment. As a matter of fact, God answered all of Moses's questions regarding his assignment.

> *But Moses protested to God, "Who am I to appear before Pharaoh? Who am I to lead the people of Israel out of Egypt?" God answered, "I will be with you. And this is your sign that I am the one who has sent you: When you have brought the people out of Egypt, you will worship God at this very mountain." But Moses protested, "If I go to the people of Israel and tell them, 'The God of your ancestors has sent me to you,' they will ask me, 'What is his name?' Then what should I tell them?" God replied to Moses, "I AM WHO I AM. Say this to the people of Israel: I AM has sent me to you." God also said to Moses, "Say this to the people of Israel: Yahweh, the God of your ancestors-the God of Abraham, the God of Isaac, and the God of Jacob-has sent me to you. This is my eternal name, my name to remember for all generations."*
> EXODUS 3:11-15 NLT

But Moses protested again, "What if they won't believe me or listen to me? What if they say, 'The Lord never appeared to you?'" Then the Lord asked him, "What is that in your hand?" "A shepherd's staff," Moses replied. "Throw it down on the ground," the Lord told him. So, Moses threw down the staff, and it turned into a snake! Moses jumped back.

Then the Lord told him, "Reach out and grab its tail." So, Moses reached out and grabbed it, and it turned back into a shepherd's staff in his hand. "Perform this sign," the Lord told him. "Then they will believe that the Lord, the God of their ancestors the God of Abraham, the God of Isaac, and the God of Jacob really has appeared to you." Then the Lord said to Moses, "Now put your hand inside your cloak." So, Moses put his hand inside his cloak, and when he took it out again, his hand was white as snow with a severe skin disease. "Now put your hand back into your cloak," the Lord said. So, Moses put his hand back in, and when he took it out again, it was as healthy as the rest of his body. The Lord said to Moses, "If they do not believe you and are not convinced by the first miraculous sign, they will be convinced by the second sign. And if they don't believe you or listen to you even after these two signs, then take some water from the Nile River and pour it out on the dry ground. When you do, the water from the Nile will turn to blood on the ground."

But Moses pleaded with the Lord, "O Lord, I'm not very good with words. I never have been, and I'm not now, even though you have spoken to me. I get tongue-tied, and my words get tangled." Then the Lord asked Moses, "Who makes a person's mouth? Who decides whether people speak or do not speak, hear or do not hear, see or do not see? Is it not I, the Lord? Now go! I will be with you as you speak, and I will instruct you in what to say." But Moses again pleaded, "Lord, please! Send anyone else." Then the Lord became angry with Moses. "All right," he said. "What about your brother, Aaron the Levite? I know he speaks well. And look! He is on his way to meet you now. He will be delighted to see you. Talk to him, and put the words in his mouth. I will be with both of you as you speak, and I will instruct you both in what to do. Aaron will be your spokesman to the people. He will be your mouthpiece,

and you will stand in the place of God for him, telling him what to say. And take your shepherd's staff with you, and use it to perform the miraculous signs I have shown you."
Exodus 4:1-17 NLT

As you can see, Moses was not a "yes man," but eventually he said yes to God. God will honor a man or woman who says yes to Him after they have seriously considered the request to serve in the Kingdom of God. God does not want an empty commitment from a person who has been asked to be the "Set Man." The Bible records the accomplishments of Moses and how he fulfilled the will of God for his life. Moses would not have been able to be successful doing the will of God if he had not seriously committed to his assignment. Moses faced the opposition of Pharaoh, the Red Sea, the wilderness experience, and the difficulty of leading God's people. But, with the help of the Lord, Moses is noted as one of the greatest leaders known to mankind.

CONVICTION FOR THE CAUSE

The Set Man must have a strong resolve and unwavering conviction to fulfill his or her godly assignment. A conviction is a fixed or firm belief that is established as truth. A conviction carries more weight than a belief. A belief is something you consider to be truth, opposed to a conviction that is something you are convinced to be the truth. A belief is something you will argue or debate about; a conviction is something you will die for. Beliefs are open for discussion, convictions are not. The Set Man must have a true conviction for his or her assignment because they will be challenged intensely to relinquish their decision to stand on their conviction.

Jesus had a strong conviction to do the will of the Father. Jesus was confronted by Satan regarding His identity and assignment in the earth.

Then Jesus was led by the Spirit into the wilderness to be tempted there by the devil. For forty days and forty nights he fasted and became very hungry. During that time, the devil came and said to him, "If you are the Son of God, tell these stones to become loaves of bread." But Jesus told him, "No! The Scriptures say, 'People do not live by bread alone, but by every word that comes from the mouth of God.'" Then the devil took him to the holy city, Jerusalem, to the highest point of the Temple, and said, "If you are the Son of God, jump off! For the Scriptures say, 'He will order his angels to protect you. And they will hold you up with their hands so you won't even hurt your foot on a stone.'" Jesus responded, "The Scriptures also say, 'You must not test the Lord your God.'" Next the devil took him to the peak of a very high mountain and showed him all the kingdoms of the world and their glory. "I will give it all to you," he said, "if you will kneel down and worship me." "Get out of here, Satan," Jesus told him. "For the Scriptures say, 'You must worship the Lord your God and serve only him.'" Then the devil went away, and angels came and took care of Jesus.

MATTHEW 4:1-11 NLT

Once a conviction is established, you will be tested to determine if your conviction is strong. Satan challenged Jesus regarding Jesus' conviction in the Father's ability to provide, protect and promote Jesus. Jesus revealed the strength of His conviction by confronting each one of Satan's questions with the Word of God. This leads us to an important Kingdom fact. Convictions regarding Kingdom matters must be founded in the Word of God. The Word of God is the only thing in life that is infallible. In God we trust, but everything else should be checked out thoroughly! Jesus would not allow Satan to distract, deceive or deny Him from accomplishing His assignment as the Set Man in the earth. Jesus gave us a prime example to follow so we will not waver in doing the will of God.

TOOLS FOR THE ASSIGNMENT

When God calls you, He will also equip you for the cause. God, in His infinite wisdom, knows that good intention without the resources to back it up is a waste of time. God gives faith for the execution of Kingdom purpose. God has given the following for Kingdom purpose: faith, wisdom, and the power of prayer.

Faith in Action:

Faith is an important tool for the set man. Faith will help you to activate the power of submission for success. Faith is trust in God that is validated by action. Every man is given faith for a purpose.

"For I say, through the grace given unto me, to every man that is among you, not to think of himself more highly than he ought to think; but to think soberly, according as God hath dealt to every man the measure of faith."

ROMANS 12:3 KJV

Faith will get things rolling in your life for the accomplishment of your Kingdom purpose. The set man must spend time developing and utilizing the measure of faith that has been given for their assignment. "Without faith, it is impossible to please God (see Hebrews 11:6)." Living by faith is a partnership between God and man which enables you to obtain what you desire and to accomplish Kingdom purpose. I learned this principle while performing a ministerial assignment.

TESTIFY

I was asked by a good friend to perform a memorial service for a family member. I live in California, but the memorial service was in Ohio. I consented to perform the memorial service; therefore, I had to fly to accomplish this request. I am tall so I needed leg room for the flight to be reasonably comfortable.

My wife worked with the airline to reserve good seats for my flight to Ohio and my return to California. The flight to Ohio went well, but on the flight back I encountered problems.

The person who arranged to pick me up for my return flight was late and consequently got me to the airport late. When I arrived at the airport, there were long lines for the identity check-in and the baggage check-in. I evaluated the possibility of making my flight on time and under the circumstances, my evaluations were more negative than positive. I wanted to scream and cuss but being a true man of God, I prayed instead.

I asked God for His help and I made the confession that I would make my flight in time. As I waited in line for the identity check, it appeared that the process was moving like slow dripping molasses. I finally completed the identity check-in, so the metal detector and baggage check were next. The line was super long and going terribly slow. I surmised that I would not have enough time to complete both checks and make my flight in time.

I again spoke to the Lord about my situation and confessed that I would make my flight in time. I was impressed in my spirit to go ask the security guard for assistance so I could skip the process. The security guard told me in a strong voice, "Get back in line!" As you can imagine, I wanted to call down the fires of heaven upon him, but I got back in line without an argument. I began to thank the Lord for His help and make the confession that I would make my flight.

Suddenly, the same security guard called me over and said, "Do not remove any of your clothing and keep your baggage and go through the metal detector." I told him, "Thank you so much," and followed his instructions. When I passed through the metal detector and arrived at the inner airport, I was ecstatic but still at risk of missing my flight.

I told the Lord, "Thank you Jesus," but I heard in my spirit, "RUN!" I was near the A1 gate, but my gate was A70. I had my briefcase and garment bag in hand, and I took off running. When I arrived at A10, I was out of breath. I have not needed to run in a while, so you can imagine my spirit was strong, but my physical man was weak. I took a brief rest, I again heard in my spirit, "RUN!" I had these episodes of stop and go all the way to gate A70. When I arrived at gate A70, I saw the last person getting on the plane. I stopped running and gathered myself, went to the gate check-in, and walked on the plane.

I had reserved seats, so my seat was available for me. I put up my garment bag in the overhead bin and sat down in my seat. I took a deep breath and asked the Lord about the whole ordeal. The Lord said to me that the experience was a lesson in faith. I said to the Lord, "How so?" The Lord said, "You asked for My help in faith, but if you did not apply action to your faith request, you would not have received your expected outcome." I told the Lord, "Thank you for the help and the lesson on faith."

The set man must be ready to respond in faith to execute the will of God. Faith is like a muscle that must be utilized and exercised on a regular basis to remain relevant and available for the cause of the Kingdom.

WISDOM FOR LEADERSHIP

Wisdom is the mind of God on what I should do. Many have equipped themselves with mast levels of knowledge, but without the wisdom of God, the application of knowledge could be a waste of time. Knowing what to do, but not knowing when to do it can leave you at risk of failure. Solomon understood this truth, which motivated him to ask God for wisdom.

> *That night the Lord appeared to Solomon in a dream, and God said, "What do you want? Ask, and I will give it to you!" Solomon replied, "You showed great and faithful love to your servant my father, David because he was honest and true and faithful to you. And you have continued to show this great and faithful love to him today by giving him a son to sit on his throne. "Now, O Lord my God, you have made me king instead of my father, David, but I am like a little child who doesn't know his way around. And here I am in the midst of your own chosen people, a nation so great and numerous they cannot be counted! Give me an understanding heart so that I can govern your people well and know the difference between right and wrong. For who by himself is able to govern this great people of yours?" The Lord was pleased that Solomon had asked for wisdom. So God replied, "Because you have asked for wisdom in governing my people with justice and have not asked for a long life or wealth or the death of your enemies I will give you what you asked for! I will give you a wise and understanding heart such as no one else has had or ever will have! And I will also give you what you did not ask for riches and fame! No other king in all the world will be compared to you for the rest of your life! And if you follow me and obey my decrees and my commands as your father, David, did, I will give you a long life."*
>
> 1 KINGS 3:5-14 NLT

Solomon felt the gravity of his assignment to be King of Israel. As the set man, Solomon was responsible for governing God's people with love and wisdom. Solomon could have asked God for strength, power, and riches. That he would be known as a powerful king who ruled with a mighty arm of authority. Solomon understood that with great power comes great responsibility in leading people. God values His people above things; therefore, leaders must value God's people and use godly wisdom when dealing with His people. Godly wisdom and good people skills are helpful qualities that enable a leader to govern appropriately. Solomon asked God for wisdom and knowledge which would help him to lead God's people in righteousness. God was so pleased with Solomon's request that he not only gave him wisdom and knowledge, but God, He also gave him wealth, possessions, and honor.

The moral of the story is that we need the wisdom of God to perform the purposes of God. Remember, to put first things first and the rest will follow. If you have the wisdom of God, God will be compelled to trust you with the power and riches of heaven.

POWER OF PRAYER FOR ACTION

Jesus told us to pray that the will of God be done in the earth. We have learned the earth belongs to God, yet He has provisioned ownership of the earth by delegating His authority to man. God has given man the responsibility to rule in the earth. This responsibility comes with the opportunity to ask for God's help. Do not be deceived, there is no way in heaven or earth that you will be able to complete the task as a set man without the help of God. All throughout the Bible, and in the experiences of mankind, we see the need for God's help to perform the task of leadership in the earth. The reason why man is relegated to live in a world full of turmoil and despair is because he refuses to pray and submit to the will of God. When mankind needs help, God has given him a direct line of communication called prayer.

> *Be careful for nothing, but in everything by prayer and supplication with thanksgiving let your requests be made known unto God.*
> Philippians 4:6 KJV

> *And it shall come to pass, that whosoever shall call on the name of the Lord shall be saved.*
> Acts 2:21 KJV

> *Then shall ye call upon me, and ye shall go and pray unto me, and I will hearken unto you.*
> Jeremiah 29:12 KJV

> *Watch and pray, that ye enter not into temptation: the spirit indeed is willing, but the flesh is weak.*
> Matthew 26:41 KJV

> *Praying always with all prayer and supplication in the Spirit, and watching thereunto with all perseverance and supplication for all saints*
> Ephesians 6:18 KJV

It is evident that prayer has the power to invite God into our daily affairs. It has been said that we must develop a "prayer life." I add to this quest that we should also develop a life of prayer. A prayer life understands a time that starts and ends, but a life of prayer is in constant connection with God, 24/7. Life happens 24/7, therefore we need to be in contact with the Master 24/7. Paul and Silas found themselves in a difficult situation that required the help of the Lord. Therefore, they commenced in a time of prayer, praise, and worship to God that produced a miracle of deliverance.

> *And at midnight Paul and Silas prayed, and sang praises unto God: and the prisoners heard them. And suddenly there was a great earthquake so that the foundations of the prison were shaken: and immediately all the doors were opened, and every one's bands were loosed.*
>
> Acts 16:25-26 kjv

As you can see, prayer ignited the supernatural intervention of God into Paul's and Silas' situation. Prayer is the power to make your problem God's problem. We all know that God is the ultimate problem solver. Prayer will invoke the power, wisdom, and help of God in times of trouble. Our natural inclination in times of trouble is to panic, but in times of trouble do not panic, instead pray! The power of prayer can change your situation. An even greater benefit of the power of prayer is that it will also change you IN the situation. Some situations will not change instantly; therefore, you may need the strength to endure like a good Christian until change comes. The Bible says, "They that wait upon the Lord will renew their strength" (see Isaiah 40:31). God does not want believers to be weak and anemic; therefore, some situations come to develop our resolve to stand in times of difficulty. The Set Man is a role model for others to follow. The power to be strong in the Lord is generated by the power of prayer.

PRAYER

Father God, you are the King and Ruler in heaven and earth. Your divine will dictate that You choose whomever You will, to lead and guide in the Kingdom of God. I submit myself to the order of the set man structure of leadership. Whoever is called to lead the vision of Your will, I humbly submit to their leadership. I understand that the appointment of Kingdom leadership comes from You. You are the omniscient One who knows all things and leads the Kingdom with Your mighty right hand of righteousness. I say, "Yes!" to Your decision and Your appointment of the Set Man. Please help me to comply with Your order and structure of leadership. In Jesus name, I pray. Amen!

CHAPTER SIX
The Support Man

The "Set Man" has been called to lead, but he or she needs support to perform their Kingdom purpose in life. The support God created for the Set Man is what I call the "Support Man." The Support Man is required to utilize their time, talent, and treasure to help the Set Man accomplish the will of God. In scripture, the Support Man is identified as the ministry of helps.

And God hath set some in the church, first apostles, secondarily prophets, thirdly teachers, after that miracles, then gifts of healings, helps, governments, diversities of tongues.
1 CORINTHIANS 12:28 KJV

The helps ministry is filled with people who have accepted the call of the Support Man. The call of the Support Man is a general call to all believers. Every person who has given their life to Christ is requested to worship and serve the Lord. The will of God is not automatically done in the earth; we must choose to support the Kingdom of God by supporting the vision.

THE VISION
It is the responsibility of every believer to join a local church, submit to the Set Man of the house and support the vision. Supporting the vision requires that you submit your heart, mind, and body to accomplish Kingdom purpose. The pastor of the church has been appointed by God to lead the ministry and ensure that the will of God is done. One of the greatest oppositions that a pastor will experience is having rebellious members who do not submit to leadership or embrace the vision of the house.

There is an ungodly manner of thinking that the Support Man does not have to submit to the Set Man because they both put their pants on the same way. Well, the way you put on your pants does not mean you are the leader! The anointing for leadership is not placed in the pants on the man; the anointing is placed on the man in the pants. Aaron and Miriam learned this when they challenged Moses' authority (see Number 12:1-16).

Aaron and Miriam surmised that Moses was not the only person God used to lead the Children of Israel. God was angry with the challenge to Moses' authority, so God made it clear to everyone that Moses was the Set Man, and all others were support men. God punished Miriam with leprosy because of her outspoken challenge to Moses' authority (see Numbers 12:1-16). God holds the vision and His chosen leader in high regard, and God expects the Support Man to do so as well.

Essentially, God gives instructions for your godly assignment through a vision. What is the vision and how can the Support Man assist the Set Man with executing the vision? God gives vision for the purpose of conveying His will and purpose for His people.

The vision defined: Vision (def):

- A reflection of what God wants to accomplish through His people to build His Kingdom in the earth

- Vision provides the following:
    - Purpose – which gives value to effort
    - Perspective – which provides motivation and understanding
    - Preparation – which ensures inevitable success
    - Promise – which is the reward of fulfilled vision

- Vision is essential "the business of the Father."

Jesus understood His purpose in the earth and declared, *"I must be about my Father's business!"*

THE DANGER OF NOT HAVING A VISION

Dissatisfaction and discouragement are not caused by the absence of things, but the absence of vision. Vision gives us focus and helps us work together to do the will of God. Order and structure are accomplished when the vision God has given becomes the priority of the day. The Word of God makes it very plain that without vision, we are like a ship without a sail.

> *Where there is no vision, the people perish:*
> *but he that keepeth the law, happy is he.*
> PROVERBS 29:18 KJV

The inference from the text is that where there is no vision the people are:
- Undisciplined – Without restraint
- Unorganized – Without structure
- Unprotected – Naked

The vision of God is accomplished by those who are invested in Kingdom purpose. We must make a conscientious effort to embrace the vision. Embracing the vision is a demonstration of using our will to partner with God and His chosen leader. We use our will for many things, but the greatest sacrifice we can make is to submit ourselves to God and to His will in the earth. We are told to love God with all our hearts, soul, and body. This is fulfilled when we are willing to make the sacrifice to execute Kingdom vision.

The accomplishment of vision is more than just a notion. To accomplish the vision, you must have three things:

1. *Desire*
2. *Preparation*
3. *Execution*

Those who wish to effectively support vision must find their place in the vision.

HOW IS VISION GIVEN?

God gives the vision to a leader. The position of the visionary is not only a position of great authority but also of great responsibility. When accomplishing the vision is unsuccessful, the leader may not be at fault, but the leader will be held responsible for the failure (i.e., Moses).

The leader is responsible for disseminating vision to the people. The people are responsible for supporting and executing vision. The part you play is important!

One of the primary reasons accomplishing vision is disrupted or placed in jeopardy of not being accomplished, is the failure to follow instructions. Even though you are eager to work for the Lord, your efforts must be submitted to His instructions.

WAIT FOR THE VISION!

I will stand upon my watch, and set me upon the tower, and will watch to see what he will say unto me, and what I shall answer when I am reproved. And the LORD answered me, and said, Write the vision, and make it plain upon tables, that he may run that readeth it. For the vision is yet for an appointed time, but at the end it shall speak, and not lie: though it tarry, wait for it; because it will surely come, it will not tarry.

HABAKKUK 2:1-3 KJV

The responsibility of the visionary is to hear from God and to ensure that the vision is documented for continual reference. The responsibility of the supporters of the vision is to wait, listen, and follow the instructions of the leader. Failure to follow instructions could waste time and ultimately become deadly (i.e., David, Uzzah, and the Ark of the Covenant). God gives vision so His people can get into position for the execution of His plan.

WHAT IS NEEDED TO GET INTO POSITION TO SUPPORT VISION

Three things you must do to position yourself to support the vision: First, you must deal with the matter of *sin*. The effect of sin is defeat, dishonor, disqualification, and death. Sin will put you in opposition to the vision. Sin, like cancer, will kill you from the inside out.

Second, you must walk in *holiness*. Holiness will protect you from the stain of sin that leads to condemnation. Walking in holiness will help you maintain a clear conscience which is needed for Kingdom ministry. Holiness will keep your mind clear of negative mindsets that counteract your desire to be pleasing to God.

Last, you must walk in *submission* to God. This book is dedicated to the concept of submission. When we submit to God, we are assigned to the Kingdom protection program. All of heaven is assigned to protect, provide, and promote the submitted believer. To submit means to come up under. When we are under heaven's rule, we are afforded everything that heaven has to offer.

The Support Man is called to be a FRIEND to the Set Man and a CHAMPION of the vision. As a friend to the Support Man, what is important to the Set Man becomes important to the Support Man. As a champion of the cause, the Support Man becomes a guardian of the vision. The Support Man must join forces with their brothers and sisters to adequately supply the assistance needed to perform their call and do the will of God.

The following five characteristics are necessary for the Support Man to execute his or her assignment with success: Faithfulness, focus, fervency, fearlessness, and a fighting spirit.

Faithfulness – the ability to be reliable and keep your word to God

Mine eyes shall be upon the faithful of the land, that they may dwell with me: he that walketh in a perfect way, he shall serve me.
PSALMS 101:6 KJV

- Faithfulness gets God's attention
- Favor finds the faithful

Focus – Keeping your actions centered on God's purpose

I press toward the mark for the prize of the high calling of God in Christ Jesus.
PHILIPPIANS 3:14 KJV

- Your focus is your guide
- When the will of God is your aim, everything else takes the backseat

Fervency – Practicing enthusiasm and excitement while performing your assignment

*I know thy works, that thou art neither cold nor hot:
I would thou wert cold or hot.*
Revelation 3:15 KJV

- Passion for God (and your assignment) will keep you fueled for the task at hand
- The five wise virgins did not let their oil run dry, so they were ready to join the Bridegroom for the celebration (Matt 25:1-13)
- God gives you oil (passion) for your assignment, not for someone else's assignment

Fearlessness – A heart of true courage and boldness

For God hath not given us the spirit of fear; but of power, and of love, and of a sound mind.
2 Timothy 1:7 KJV

- Fear will keep you on the sidelines of ineffectiveness and shame
- Courage will cause you to get in the game and produce on a high level
- Power, love, and a sound mind (self-control) are the formula for fearlessness

　　Without Power – You have no impact

　　Without Love – Power will be misused

　　Without a sound mind – Love can be taken advantage of

A Fighting Spirit – The ability to outlast the enemy

I have fought a good fight, I have finished my course, I have kept the faith:
2 Timothy 4:7 kjv

- A fighting spirit will cause you to stand in the face of adversity
- The Bible declares that *We are more than conquerors.* (Romans 8:37) In other words, we not only win in life, but we win overwhelmingly
- The reason we can fight with such confidence is because God is on our side

Fear thou not; for I am with thee: be not dismayed; for I am thy God: I will strengthen thee; yea, I will help thee; yea, I will uphold thee with the right hand of my righteousness.
Isaiah 41:10 kjv

- How can you lose with this power that you use – The Power of God

God gives us the power to finish our assignment and to overcome all opposition from the enemy.

THE POWER OF GOD FOR THE ASSIGNMENT

And they overcame him by the blood of the Lamb, and by the word of their testimony, and they loved not their lives unto the death.
Revelation 12:11 kjv

To have the strength to fight against the enemy and the oppositions of the flesh, we must learn to use our Kingdom weapons.

THE WEAPONS OF WARFARE

1. The Blood of The Lamb
   The Blood of The Lamb gives us three things:
   - I. Purchase Power – Everything belongs to God therefore you can use the Blood to obtain the resources necessary for your assignment
   - II. Protective Power – God is our source of protection
   - III. Penetrating Power – God's power will break every chain of the enemy

2. The Word of Our Testimony
   - I. Our testimony is filled with confidence, assurance, and expectation
   - II. David overcame Goliath with a testimony

3. The Sacrifice of Their Lives (Love not their lives unto death)
   - I. The investment of your life signifies trust and faith in God
   - II. Faith in God releases the supernatural power of God for your assignment
   - III. The supernatural will help you overcome the enemy and finish your "godly assignment"

Application of Kingdom resources is appropriated through prayer. We must utilize the power of prayer to activate the weapons of warfare. Just knowing what to do is not good enough, we must incorporate the power of prayer along with the Word of God to get Kingdom results.

THE POWER OF PRAYER

We are called to stand against the enemy with the power of prayer.

Prayer (def):
- Prayer is personal and corporate communication with God
- Prayer is a spiritual connection with God, that enables a transfer of God's wisdom, grace, and power in your life

One of the strongest powers in the earth is COMMUNICATION (OR PRAYER); that is why God requires us to pray so that we can be fueled with the Power of Prayer for purpose.

God destroyed the Tower of Babel project by disrupting their ability to communicate (Satan is using that strategy with the saints).

THE BENEFITS OF PRAYER

1. Prayer will open you to a spirit of discernment so you can be in sync with what God is doing in the earth. It is critical that we submit to God's will, way, and timing.
2. Prayer will keep you in position for an open heaven.
3. Prayer activates faith for Kingdom living.

Standing Against Adversity

> *Therefore take up the whole armor of God, that you may be able to withstand in the evil day, and having done all, to stand.*
> EPHESIANS 6:12-18 NKJV

- According to this scripture, the believer's stand must be a "prayer stand."
- The believer's effectiveness in prayer relies on their being equipped with the armor of God.

THE PRAYER ARMOR

Belt of Truth – Truth is the foundation for godly living. *And you shall know the truth, and the truth shall make you free.* (John 8:32 NKJV)

Breast Plate of Righteousness – Righteousness protects the condition of your heart and soul (out of your heart flows the power for righteous living). The breastplate protects the heart from deceit, deception, and destruction.

> How do we protect our hearts? By monitoring our eyes, our mouth, and our feet. They are gateways to our heart and souls

Shoes of Peace – Peace is the right relationship between God and man based on the gospel. Walking in peace will allow God to compel your enemies to be at peace with you.

Shield of Faith – Faith quenches all the fiery darts (fear, unbelief, and doubt) of the enemy.

Helmet of Salvation – Salvation protects your mind from lethal thoughts that derail you.

Sword of The Spirit – The Word of God is your sword of offense and defense against the enemy.

Prayer – Prayer is your standing position in spiritual warfare.

THE PRAYER ARMOR IS AN ESSENTIAL KEY FOR THE BELIEVERS VICTORY

- Jesus said man should always pray and not give up, lose heart, or faint. (see Luke 18:1 KJV)
- Jesus said to his disciples, *The spirit is willing, but the flesh is weak—pray that ye might not fall into temptation."* (Matthew 26:41 KJV)

When we pray, we invite a heaven response to our situation!

PRAYER POWER

Confess your trespasses to one another, and pray for one another, that you may be healed. The effective, fervent prayer of a righteous man avails much.

JAMES 5:16 NKJV

- Prayer generates strength, ability, and force for change and deliverance

WHEN YOU PRAY:

1. God will go to work on your behalf. Prayer makes your problem God's problem, *Casting all your care upon him; for he careth for you.* (1 Peter 5:7 KJV)
2. Angels are released to fight on your behalf.
3. Obstacles are removed from your purpose and destiny.
4. The impossible becomes possible (with man it is impossible, with God all things are possible)!
5. The supernatural is released for supernatural results!

We have the promise of God to help us if we pray.

The Support Man

If My people who are called by My name will humble themselves, and pray and seek My face, and turn from their wicked ways, then I will hear from heaven, and will forgive their sin and heal their land.
                                                CHRONICLES 7:14 NKJV

When you pray, God will:
- Hear you
- Forgive you
- Heal you
- Empower you

Samson prayed and invited the power of God to help him fulfill his assignment in fighting the enemies of God. Prayer changes things!

The expectation of the Kingdom of God is results. When the Set Man and the Support Man work together to fulfill Kingdom vision, they are an unstoppable force in the earth. When evil men worked together to build the tower of Babel, God made it known that success was imminent. If evil men have the power to generate an effort to execute ungodly agenda, the Children of God will be unstoppable when they work together in the spirit of submission to execute the Kingdom agenda.

PRAYER

Father God, You have called me to support the vision and to submit to Kingdom leadership. Your will and Your way are holy and require complete obedience and compliance. Lord, I ask You to help me do what is necessary to contribute to Your holy cause. Lord, please help me to deal with anything that blocks me from supporting Your will and the Set Man. Please help me to deal with the sin in my life. Please help me to walk in holiness and in submission to Your authority. I ask all these things in Jesus' name. Amen!

CHAPTER SEVEN

Walking in Submission

*And we know that all things work together for good to them that love
God, to them who are the called according to his purpose.*

Roman 8:28 kjv

We have come to the end of our journey in exploring the necessity to develop a heart of submission. The heart of submission keeps us connected to our Father and puts us in a place of value-added service to the Kingdom of God. When we submit our lives to God, we can expect to become productive members in the Kingdom of God. The expectation of the Kingdom of God is Kingdom results. The results expected are in line with the purposes of God. We cannot just conjure up ideas, suggestions, and activities to submit to the plan of God. We must walk in accordance with the will of God. The purpose and will of God must be our guide.

*After this manner, therefore, pray ye: Our Father which
art in heaven, Hallowed be thy name. 10Thy kingdom come.
Thy will be done in earth, as it is in heaven.*

Matthew 6:9-10 kjv

The Kingdom of God is the rule and reign of God in the hearts of men, women, and children. The Kingdom of Heaven is the rule and reign of God in the earth (The establishment and manifestation of His governments). The rule of God is expressed when we submit ourselves in obedience to His will and His way. Jesus submitted Himself to the will of the Father, which provided the perfect example for those who are connected to the Kingdom of God.

WHY WAS MAN CREATED?

Man was created by God with purpose, on purpose, for purpose. The PURPOSE of life is a life of PURPOSE. When purpose is not known, abuse is inevitable. When you discover the WHY for life, the WHEN, WHAT, WHERE, and HOW for living will reveal themselves. Purpose for living starts with God.

> *The Lord will fulfill his PURPOSE for me; your steadfast love, O Lord, endures forever. Do not forsake the work of your hands.*
> PSALMS 138:8 ESV

The purpose for life starts with three things:
1. Knowing God – Relationship with God (not religion or practicing rules).
2. Loving God – Commitment to God.
3. Worshipping (Serving) God – Honoring God with your life and service.

The Purpose for mankind is revealed in the book of beginnings.

> *And God said, Let us make man in our image, after our likeness: and let them have dominion over the fish of the sea, and over the fowl of the air, and over the cattle, and over all the earth, and over every creeping thing that creepeth upon the earth.*
> GENESIS 1:26-28 KJV

- Man was created by God to be a holy representative of God's glory and power in the earth.
- God made man in His image (to look like God), and in His likeness (to act like God).
  - How do we express God's image? Be holy, be loving, be righteous, be creative.
  - How do we express God's likeness? Walk-in authority, walk-in power, walk-in wisdom.
  - Essentially, we are to live like God in the earth with the same authority, the same power, and with the same results.

There are tangible benefits available when we agree to live a life of Kingdom purpose.

> *And we know that all things work together for good to them that love God, to them who are the called according to his purpose.*
> ROMANS 8:28 KJV

THE BENEFITS OF LIVING A LIFE OF PURPOSE
1. Purpose brings focus to your life – eliminates confusion.
2. Purpose establishes value of living – you are not a mistake.
3. Purpose will move you to fulfillment of destiny – causes inevitable success.
4. Purpose will make you appealing and attractive to others – you will be a godly influence.
5. Purpose will cause not enough, to become more than enough – you will command Kingdom supply (Jesus fed 5000).
6. Purpose will cause your enemies to work on your behalf – supernatural favor.

7. Purpose will help you make a positive impact – the Kingdom will be advanced.

WHAT IS NECESSARY TO FIND PURPOSE

He saith unto them, But whom say ye that I am? And Simon Peter answered and said, Thou art the Christ, the Son of the living God. And Jesus answered and said unto him, Blessed art thou, Simon Barjona (Jonah's Son): for flesh and blood hath not revealed it unto thee, but my Father which is in heaven. And I say also unto thee, That thou art Peter, and upon this rock I will build my church; and the gates of hell shall not prevail against it. And I will give unto thee the keys of the kingdom of heaven: and whatsoever thou shalt bind on earth shall be bound in heaven: and whatsoever thou shalt loose on earth shall be loosed in heaven.

MATTHEW 16:15-19 KJV

WHAT YOU NEED IS REVELATION

1. Revelation of who God is
2. Revelation of who you are
3. Revelation of your authority . . . (authority is given because of responsibility and purpose)

HOW DO YOU OBTAIN REVELATION?

1. By the Word of God
2. By the power of the Holy Spirit
3. By walking in faith in God

When you know your PURPOSE in life, you have the knowledge to overcome anyone or anything that comes to block you from fulfilling purpose. Circumstances do not determine purpose, God's word and will determine purpose. David knew his purpose in life; therefore, his family, his enemies, and circumstances could not stop him from his destiny. Samuel was instructed by God to go to Jesse's house to find the next King of Israel. Jesse brought before Samuel seven sons that he believed could be God's choice. Man's choice is usually different than God's choice. Man looks on the outside, but God looks one the inside where purpose is deposited.

> *Then Samuel asked, "Are these all the sons you have?" "There is still the youngest," Jesse replied. "But he's out in the fields watching the sheep and goats." "Send for him at once," Samuel said. "We will not sit down to eat until he arrives."*
> 1 SAMUEL 16:11 NLT

A great observation in this scripture is that purpose usually finds those who have a mind to work. David was in the field performing his assigned task when he was summonsed for his Kingdom purpose. Do not be dismayed if you have been given the opportunity to perform the thing that you know God assigned to you. Just keep moving forward in action and you will walk right into your purposed position.

> *So Jesse sent for him. He was dark and handsome, with beautiful eyes. And the LORD said, "This is the one; anoint him." So as David stood there among his brothers, Samuel took the flask of olive oil he had brought and anointed David with the oil. And the Spirit of the LORD came powerfully upon David from that day on. Then Samuel returned to Ramah.*
> 1 SAMUEL 16:12-13 NLT

HEART OF SUBMISSION

David was selected by God to be king, not because of what was on the outside, but for what was on the inside (he was made to be king). When you are selected by God for purpose, He will appoint you and anoint you!

Purpose Will Release:
- Position for your assignment
- Provision for your assignment
- Power for your assignment

Another keynote observation as to why David eventually moved to his place of purpose, was because David was a worshipper, warrior, and a winner! Worship will bring you and keep you in the face of God. In the face of God is where we receive our assignment for purpose and the ability and power to perform our Kingdom purpose. When you worship God, He deposits Himself into your life and helps you to walk out His will in the earth. There are countless men and women who were known worshippers and provided a testimony of victory?

THOSE WHO WALKED IN PURPOSE

a) Noah walked in purpose and saved his family from the flood
b) Moses walked in purpose and delivered his family from Egypt
c) Esther walked in purpose and saved her people from genocide
d) Jesus walked in purpose and became the Savior of the world

We were created to live for God and walk in Kingdom purpose. In order for man to accomplish this goal in life, we must develop a heart of submission. When we submit our lives to God, we can expect to begin a journey of successful living, which brings glory to God, joy in our hearts, and a testimony that will inspire others to do the same.

Stand strong in the Lord and I call you blessed!

PRAYER

Father God, knowing Your will and walking in Kingdom purpose is a requirement for the believer; therefore, I ask that You help me to find my place inside Your holy purpose for my life. I ask that You speak to me regarding my purpose through Your word and by the Holy Spirit. Lord, help me to become like David who was a worshipper, warrior, and winner. I understand the heart of submission positions me appropriately to be available for Your will and Your way. Father God, I give you my heart, soul, and body so that You can use me whenever, wherever, for whatever You desire. I love you Lord, and I ask for all these things in Jesus' name. Amen!

About the Author

**SYLVESTER BELL
HEART OF SUBMISSION**

Sylvester Bell is a respected leader in the Christian community. He is a loving husband and father, a ministry pastor, and a submitted servant who has dedicated his life to God.

Sylvester Bell has served as a ministry Pastor at Living Praise Christian Church for over 20 years. He also serves as one of LPCC's iServe Ministry of Helps Directors, and he also serves as a Council member for LPCC's Men's group called Men of Valor & Excellence (MOVE).

Sylvester Bell is a true believer who has developed a lasting relation with the Lord. Throughout his life he has experienced success and failure which has taught him that submission to God is the key to a life of great joy and happiness.

One of Sylvester's life goals is to share his testimony and life journey with others so that they can gleam revelation and principles that lead to a life that is pleasing to God.

Printed in Great Britain
by Amazon